The End of Selling.......
as we know it

An executive's guide to customer creation

by Larry Welke

1stBooks – rev. 2/19/01

Dedication

To Niserella, my not so secret love.

Table of Contents

Acknowledgments

The first person I need to thank is my 7th Grade teacher at Dover St. School on the southside of Milwaukee, Mrs. Moody. One day, handing back my homework, she said, "Someday, write a book." I'd not thought about doing that up to that point in my life — like most 12 year olds, I had other things on my mind. Nonetheless the thought stayed with me.

I am also indebted to the many, many individuals who labored through my sales training classes for the eleven plus years they were held. As is so often the case, the teacher learned as much or more than the taught.

And I owe at least a comment to Dennis Hamilton, once and always my editor-in-chief. God only knows why he puts up with me. And another comment for Angela Butler, the faithful and patient woman who took my scribbling and converted it into readable text.

Most of all I must thank my wife Janice, for two years of listening to me promise to write — and finish — this book. Without her encouraging words and support, this book would still be idle chatter at a cocktail party.

Preface

The End of Selling is not just an attempt at a catchy book title; it's a reality for those involved in the complex transaction — both buyer and seller. As a person charged with the responsibility of creating customers for your organization, it's also possibly the best news you can get, an opportunity of a lifetime — or at least of a career.

Sales, selling, salesmanship — arguably if not the oldest then the second oldest profession in the world — has changed substantially over the history of commercial activity. Based originally on nothing more than scarcity and a difference in perceived value — I have something you don't have but you think it is more valuable than I do — the act of selling has since become a discipline surrounded by too much folklore on the one hand, and not enough thoughtful science on the other.

Because we seek to understand the world around us, to make it both known and predictable, there is a great tendency to rationalize those things that we don't understand. That allows us to fit them into a common comfort level which then becomes a belief system, shared by many if not most. The people directly involved in selling, as well as the general public, all too often operate on that belief system with a corrupting consequence to the sales profession.

Before we get too deeply involved in the adventure of selling, pause for a moment to take a pop-quiz. The following 12 statements reflect a belief system about selling. Identify those you feel — or know — to be true, and those that you feel are patently false. As with the rest of this book, the statements are not offered as secular scripture nor should your answers be regarded as moral imperatives. It is more a matter of what you believe, whether from first-or second-hand experience, hearsay or heresy.

TRUE or FALSE?

1. Sales people are different; not everybody can sell. F
2. Military terms best describe sales activity — it IS a battlefield out there. F
3. A good salesperson will always control the sales situation; that's one of the characteristics of a good salesperson. F

4. The harder a salesperson works, the more likely he is to succeed.
5. A salesperson has to learn to not take rejection personally.
6. Pareto's Law applies to sales as well as to everything else: 80% of sales will be generated by 20% of the sales force. That's just the way it is.
7. It's tough to keep a good attitude when you know you'll be rejected 19 out of 20 times.
8. It's best to hire only experienced sales people.
9. Building a relationship takes a lot of time and effort and doesn't always pay off.
10. Close early; close often. Buyers expect that and you'll be rewarded with increased sales.
11. Business-to-business selling is a matter of price/performance, not personality.
12. With today's well-informed and sophisticated market, the rational reasons to buy are now more important than any emotional appeal.

There was a time, not that long ago, when all 12 of those statements were accepted as gospel truth. Sales VPs lived — or died — by them; compensation plans were built on their truth; organizations were structured on their applicability. Some companies practiced these laws religiously with consequent success and others violated them with fervor with the same consequent success.

What's going on? How can that be? Well, as with so many things in life, each of the 12 can be true - or false. You don't lose if your answer should have been the other; you just work harder and probably spend more time before you achieve any level of success. While there still may be anecdotal truth to some of them, for the business-to- business complex sale, the case can be made for the falsity of all. Think about them, one by each:

1. *Sales people are different; not everybody can sell.* If sales people are different, how are they different? Physically? Educationally? Emotionally? Geographically? No, in truth, anyone who wants to be an accountant can be one, or an engineer, auto mechanic, or salesperson. The desire to be is the only thing that makes a salesperson different from another. Being people-oriented is a nice

quality also, but that's a quality shared by engineers, auto mechanics and even some accountants.

Neither the desire to sell nor a people-orientation are differentiators to set sales people apart. Anyone who takes the time and effort to understand the practice of selling can be successful at it, regardless of age, sex, color, religion or any other known means of classifying the human animal.

2. *Military terms best describe sales activity — it IS a battlefield out there.* Military terms *can* be used to describe sales activity — but is that what *best* describes it? Military terms like: enemy, beat, kill, force, all set the stage for an adversarial relationship. Some businesses choose to operate in that environment, with the attendant emotion and conflict stimuli. To the extent that military terms are used and become the culture of the organization, behavior and attitude will follow the same pattern.

Can that be a successful environment? Sure. Self-sustaining? As long as management can cause the vision of an enemy to be conquered. When that falters, we end up with a Viet Nam War, where there is no real or accepted consensus to the reason we're out here knocking ourselves out, our friends think we're a bit dippy for what we're doing and even our victories are Pyrrhic at best. The business of selling might have been on a battlefield long ago. Now it's a dance. Let the music begin.

3. *A good salesperson will always control the sale situation: that's one of the characteristics of a good salesperson.* The easiest way to evaluate the need for a salesperson to control is to take the position of the buyer. The last time you were a buyer of anything, and the salesperson assumed — or even attempted — control, how did you feel? Did you like that? Was it comfortable? Did you buy anything?

If we don't like being controlled when we're buyers, why do we teach our sales staff they ought to be in control? To know where you're going, to lead, to aid, yes. Where is the need for control? Anyway, control is an illusion whose source is doubt and fear. That's hardly the bedrock of successful selling.

4. *The harder a salesperson works, the more likely he is to succeed.* It's not the *harder* a person works; it's the *smarter* a person works. The most successful sales people I know will admit they're not working very hard — but they are enjoying what they're doing. And they might do it more than between eight to five, and they might do it on weekends and they don't lead very structured lives in the sense the rest of the civilized world does.

Sales people at their best are knowledge workers. Mental activity is more important than physical activity; attitude takes precedence to movement; quality ranks over quantity; and consistency no longer is the refuge of the totally unimaginative. It becomes the basis for trust and hence growth of the relationship.

5. *A salesperson has to learn to not take rejection personally.* Does a salesperson really have to learn to not take rejection personally? And, if so, how does one do that? Rejection, after all, is rejection. To not be affected by it would require some kind of disposition aberrant to the human animal. Good sales people are also sensitive people. They can hurt just like real people hurt. They might not show it as easily as some, but the sting is felt no matter how thick the hide.

Rather than attempting to de-personalize rejection, why not remove the possibility of it? We each create the situation that leads to rejection; if we stop doing that, it stands to reason we will no longer be rejected. Unless you're into S & M behavior patterns, why not stop creating the opportunity for it?

6. *Pareto's Law applies to sales as well as to everything else: 80% of sales will be generated by 20% of the sales force. That's just the way it is.* Vilfredo Pareto was an Italian economist who, in 1923, made a statement about income distribution seeming to be independent from government policy. He noted that 80% of the income in many countries is earned by just 20% of the people regardless of what the government was doing with tax policy, etc. That was a generalization, but at the same time a limited statement.

It wasn't Vilfredo who applied the 80/20 to all possible phenomena; it was the idle of the world who jumped at the opportunity to excuse their lack of action by claiming, "That's just the way it is".

If indeed 20% of your sales force generates 80% of your revenue stream, either train the remaining 80% of the sales force or fire them. Do you think for a minute that if you did, then 20% of the remaining would generate 80% of the revenue?

Assigning poor performance to Pareto's Law is just sloppy thinking. To begin with, "Law" is a misnomer. It's not a Law, it was an observation, a "seems-to-be-the-case", not a scientifically proven rule. It's a handy knee-jerk defense that allows the user to get out of the room before another question is put on the table. The next time someone uses it on you, challenge them and put a bet on the answer. Do that often enough and you'll be rich. Friendless possibly, but rich.

7. *It's tough to keep a good attitude when you know you'll be rejected 19 out of 20 times.* This has been answered already. Why would anyone put themselves in the position to be rejected 19 out of 20 times? The fear of this happening is what causes sales people to not prospect, to wait for the phone to ring, in short to be reactive rather than pro-active. They only need to learn to not set themselves up for the rejection — to prevent it from happening in the first place. Life can be beautiful.

8. *It's best to hire only experienced sales people.* Oh? If you hire only experienced people you not only end up paying more money than you need to, you also have the pleasure of overcoming all the baggage they bring with them from all the experience they've had. Inexperienced people bring no baggage, are lower cost, are usually more eager and there are more of them. Yes, you have to train them, but if you then treat them right, you have lifetime employees.

That's not to say one should *not* hire experienced sales people. The keyword was "only". Experienced or inexperienced, use the three-point approach: hire selectively, train thoroughly, cull quickly. It only takes one person to make a dysfunctional family, team or department.

9. *Building a relationship takes a lot of time and effort and doesn't always pay off.* Building a relationship takes a lot of time and effort — and it doesn't always pay off. And the converse is also true. As the sage said: If you think you can or if you think you can't, you're right. Besides, what's so difficult about building a relationship? People like likable people. Just be one of those. And even if it doesn't work out, what have you lost? You didn't have anything to start with so the most you're out is your effort. Truth be known, if you put enough effort into it, you wouldn't be out that, either.

10. *Close early; close often. Buyers expect that and you'll be rewarded with increased sales.* Again, this is not rocket science. What is your reaction when a salesperson tries to get your OK before you're ready? Before you understand what you're getting yourself into? Before all your questions are answered? Before you've integrated all the implications and consequences of the transaction into your needs and alternatives? Sales people who 'close early, close often' are what gives selling a bad name. Buyers probably do expect that — from novice sales people, from low price/low value, single call/single decision maker sales situations. But from a professional salesperson involved in a complex transaction the only reward would likely be the hallway leading to the EXIT sign.

11. *Business-to-business selling is a matter of price/performance, not personality.* This is the typical half-truth that passes for the whole truth because we parse the words and not the thought. Business-to-business selling *is* a matter of price/performance — but the performance includes more than the performance of the item being purchased. It also includes the performance of the company that is selling the item, and the performance of the salesperson.

Likewise, the price of the transaction includes the cost of the item as well as the cost (dollars and psychic) of dealing with this supplier and its representative. To deny personality has a role in business-to-business selling is to deny that people are involved in the sale. If people *can* be removed from the transaction, they will be. Then the personality is also removed. Until the person is removed the personality remains.

12. *With today's well-informed and sophisticated market, the rational reasons to buy are now more important than any emotional appeal.* The argument can easily be made that just the converse could be true — that because the market does have more information and is more sophisticated, the emotional appeal will be the competitive advantage that makes the sale. The rational reason is always necessary because the buyer can't tell the boss that the decision was made based on emotion. But, then, do we buy from people we don't like? Not unless there is no choice. In today's marketplace we have more than enough choice, even if one of them is only "not now."

As was said at the beginning, the evidence of truth in any of the 12 statements is solely in the eye of the beholder. Believing them to be true will not prevent you from being successful in sales. It will only cause you to work harder with less to show for it.

The rest of this book is devoted to a discussion of selling and buying and people who sell and buy and others who buy and sell and how the whole process can be really enjoyable and beneficial for all concerned. The discussion is about rules and tools, new ways to examine and evaluate that which has changed and that which has not.

Sales, selling, salesmanship are neither difficult nor arcane. There's no magic to it, black or otherwise. Selling has been going on for thousands of years and will continue for thousands more. In addition to originally being based on scarcity and a difference in perceived value, selling also had involved a lack of knowledge, usually on the part of the buyer, sometimes due to the deceptive practices of the seller.

In today's information-rich world, only haste or carelessness can account for an uninformed buyer. Indeed, *caveat emptor* may well be replaced with *caveat venditor* thanks in no small part to the rise of the

Internet in daily life. Access to information has contributed to the shift in role for both buyer and seller. So has the pace of change, and the price of error.

Insanity was once described as a person who does the same thing over and over and expects a different result each time. If you are doing the same thing over and over in an attempt to create a customer and you are pleased with your result — whatever that may be, save yourself the time and cost of reading this book.

If on the other hand you sense the possibility of improving your performance by changing what you are doing, continue on. It's not a long book; it's not bulked up with anecdotes and examples. The text is direct, somewhat blunt, maybe even controversial for some. But it's tried and marketplace proven. And your customers will love you for it.

But we're getting ahead of the story.

Chapter 1

Yet Another Book on Selling?

Does the world really need yet another tome on 'How to Sell'? There are dozens already, each more detailed than the last, or with a new angle, approach or technique. And it was inevitable, given our pollster-driven social structure, that the latest books would be based on a 'recent national survey' and interviews with 15,000 sales people.

Nonetheless, the answer to the basic question is: yes, we probably should continue writing and reading about creating customers — not because the previous books didn't get it right, but because the world of commerce continues to change and in many cases the practice of *customer creation* has not. The previous books were, in many cases, of great help in defining the then needed rituals, strictures and structures of sales. But when your competitor becomes your target customer, when integration becomes more important than quality, when the delivery system (read: packaging, financing, support, installation and fulfillment) become more important than the generic product or service being sold, then what was called selling, of economic necessity, must be changed.

The essence of creating a customer is communication, the transfer of information sufficient to cause a transaction to take place. The advantage had always favored the seller, who seemed to know more than the buyer about the product/service being offered as well as the problem allegedly being solved. But now, there are three major changes taking place that will forever change the nature of commerce, and cause the end of selling as we have known it. Not too surprisingly, all three have to do with information.

1. The rate of technology change in almost every industry exceeds the learning curve of the buyer. Ten years ago corporate computer software buyers wanted assurance that the vendor had a plan in place for upgrading its software product. In today's market, any upgrade plan that brings out new releases of the software more frequently than every 18-24 months will probably receive demerits. Because of too frequent upgrades, total cost of

ownership can be as much as three times the cost of the generic software product.

Nor is it merely a matter of staying on top of the technology you've bought. The technology you didn't buy is also changing. Although all the necessary information is more available than ever before, the constraint is available time. Product cycles are shorter; trained personnel are as scarce as moose eggs; and competition has never been better or more plentiful. Meanwhile, time remains uni-directional and somehow anchored to the spin of the earth.

2. Additionally, it's difficult to think of a category of product these days where the feature/function set does not exceed the expectation of the prospect. For instance, I use about 12 % of the available functionality of my word processing software. I dare say, you use about the same. It might be a different 12% but the point is there's still 88% you don't need. The same is true of cars, many home appliances and office products and, increasingly, financial services.

Whether the increased feature/functionality was designed to broaden the market or to beat the competition, the net result was to remove feature/function from the list of decision-making criteria for buying the product/service. If everyone has the needed features, what's to choose?

3. And, finally, the ubiquity of the Internet and its ability to provide any needed information on a 24 x 7 schedule minimizes if not eliminates the need for the sales person whose only value-add is feature/function knowledge. That information can be supplied on-line, by kiosk or ATM, inter — or intra — net, for far less cost than using error prone humans.

So what's the default procedure when faced with doing the unknown, all the usual metrics no longer apply, and talking to the sales rep is about as productive as talking to a machine? That's the end of selling as we know it. If you're charged with the task of creating customers for your enterprise, the next hundred plus pages will explain how your world has changed and what you need to do to change with it. Mind you, it's not absolutely necessary for you to change — failure, after all, is an equal opportunity sport.

To save readers some time, let's start with what this book will NOT accomplish:

1. *Anyone looking for a quick fix to spike sales should look elsewhere.* This book will not be your silver bullet. If you're 30% of annual quota and its December 15th, you have a different kind of problem than what this book addresses. Quick fixes in sales, belong with needles and pills, with those involved suffering the predictable but uncomfortable consequences.

Now, if it's January 15 and you want to ensure your making quota for the year, read on — help is on the way.

2. *This book will not provide you with the winning dialogue that guarantees the sale.* A good number of How-to-Sell books read like semantic primers or the script of a B-movie. It's the memorized Q&A approach: if the client says this, then you say that, and if the client doesn't say that then you say this. These are the same books that not only identify the 67 ways to 'close' but give them names as well - the Little Professor Close, the Soap Opera Close, the Yes, But Close, *ad infinitum (*or *nauseum)*. The problem with memorized dialog is that it interferes with who you as a salesperson really are. If you willfully prevent your being yourself, you become a phony. Why should anyone trust you then? First trust yourself; then others can easily follow your lead.

3. *If you're looking for the complex and difficult answer to a complex and difficult problem, once again you've come to the wrong place.* As has often been said: If you think you can, or if you think you can't, you're right. We've taken the view that creating customers is not only easy, it's enjoyable, fun, rewarding, a great way to spend a lifetime.

There seems to be a natural tendency for any discipline to develop its own unwritten rules, language and mythology. That's true of the legal profession, accountants, sailors and some try to apply it to this profession as well. In reality, it is more common sense than rocket science, more heart and head than quadratic equations. If you want to make it appear difficult to impress your spouse, neighbor or boss, that's a game you can play, but know deep down inside that it's only as tough as you choose to make it.

4. *And lastly, reading, indeed studying and/or memorizing this book will not make anyone a successful salesperson — unless they want to be one and were headed in that direction anyhow.* Being successful is a two-edged proposition. Not only is a desire necessary, but the desire must be so strong a force as to cause the person to change and accommodate the resulting success. New activity patterns will emerge; new priorities will push their way forward; old behaviors will interfere with new opportunities. Choices will have to be made.

Sorting out the answers to all the new alternatives available is sometimes the most difficult part of success. However, don't confuse struggling with actually doing something. Selling success is different than what you do with the success once you have it. Odds are, if you have succeeded consciously — that is, if you are aware of what you've done, what you're doing, and what remains to be done — then dealing with the consequent result will merely be a continuation of the process. Success does breed success.

Having said all that, what is the purpose of this book? There are six purposes in total, all basic, aimed at those people who want to excel in the activity of their marketplace. One or several might be more important to one person than to another. Consequently, they are offered in no logical sequence with no presumed priority.

1. *The first purpose is to clarify the traditional role of selling and its relationship to commerce.* A long time ago, someone purportedly said: Nothing happens until someone sells something. That might not have been true for hunter/gatherers, possibly not true in early agrarian society. However as specialization occurred, and scarcity economics came to be formulated, the need to trade, barter or sell became commonplace and the truth of the statement became evident.

Information, or rather, the lack of equal access to information, often determined relative value of what was being sold. Perceived scarcity determined price as much as feature/function and sellers took pains to withhold rather than share information that might lower their price. That's the laissez faire system that we all have come to know and maybe love.

The early days of the telegraph and telephone served the seller more so than the buyer but the advent of radio, television and now the Internet has shifted the balance significantly to the buyer. It's difficult to imagine a product or service that today need be bought in ignorance. Information abounds. Today, the basic statement might be changed to: Nothing happens until something is bought. That would reflect some of the change taking place as automation further invades the marketplace.

To further clarify, note the three very general types or categories of sales:

a) There are a certain number and type of products that can be classed as impulse or **commodity items**. Not much, if any, information is needed for the buyer; the purchase is relatively trivial (at least in the buyer's frame of reference) or has little perceived unknown consequence. Increasingly these items are bought through ATMs, kiosks, catalogs and/or on-line (the Internet). The challenge for the producer is one of marketing and distribution rather than conventional selling. The buyer knows what he/she wants; it is often an item that has been bought before; in many cases it is considered a commodity — by buyer, seller, or both.

b) There are **products and services** that require no more than one call, to one decision-maker, are low priced and do not require installation or training to use. For want of a better term they would be called **simple transactions**. The category includes many basic types of office machines, some software (most shrink-wrapped), and a lot of home appliances. This category is dependent in large part on sales effort by people well trained on the product and its competition. Success is often a matter of being best-of-breed or best price, and the prospect, in many cases, has come to the seller.

c) Lastly, there are those multiple-call, higher-priced, multiple decision-maker products and services where feature/function might be less important than its delivery system (service, support, installation, financing as well as physical fulfillment). That's termed a **complex transaction**. It has a longer sales cycle, economics are mixed with politics and invariably the person paying the bill does not understand the technology being bought.

In real life, the three categories become many more because there are an infinite number of variables that make the transaction more or less simple or complex.

What is being described in this book is primarily aimed at the complex transaction. It can be applied to the impulse item and the simple transaction as well, but only with caution and an open mind. Impulse and simple transactions are still more subject to feature/function selling techniques than the personal and social competencies of the salesperson, but that doesn't mean sales success could not be improved if the salesperson upgraded his or her approach. For that to happen usually requires sales management to first change their practices as well as their objectives and goals. Those that look at the sales function as a task of only getting the order are short changing the power and potential of their staff.

2. *Another purpose of the book is to describe and define the changing relationship of the elements involved in customer creation.* For complex sales these are: seller, buyer, selling company, product/service being proposed, and market. The salesperson chooses all of these by dint of choosing one company or product to represent over another. What many then forget is that the choice is not an event, it's an on-going process.

Relationship selling is initially thought of in terms of the relationship between buyer and seller. Well and good, that might even be the most important relationship - but it's only one of seven, any of which will be the most important at a given moment in time.

The complex sale not only involves multiple people on the buyers side of the equation; there are multiple people on the sellers side as well - technical support staff, installation and conversion help, management, accountants and probably lawyers in some instances. The person responsible for creating the customer is the most likely point person for all these contacts.

Add to that list the product manager for what is being sold. Any salesperson who doesn't establish — and curry — that relationship is forgetting which side of the bread has spread, and by whom. That's not to say every salesperson can/should/will petition changes to the product to suit what was promised to the client. But it is to say that having the inside track on planned product features won't hurt, that recognizing the talent behind the product is worth the small effort required.

The salesperson's relationship to the market involves knowing the competition, the trade associations (if any), the trade shows, the concerned press. It means participating as a speaker, possibly contributing as a writer, attending industry functions. It means being visible.

Each of the elements involved in successful selling can be used to further the sales process. Determining the part each plays, when and how, is part of the salesperson's responsibility. What is critical to understand is that the availability of information is dramatically affecting the entire process of the complex sale — and the process will continue to change to where we no longer refer to the activity as selling; rather, it's a matter of creating customers.

3. *To approach the above elements on a random or ad hoc basis could overwhelm even a senior experienced sales rep.* That gives rise to the third purpose of this book: to develop an organized, structured methodology to get people through the process, taking them from contact to first contract, and beyond. Creating customers in the long term is not an accidental/incidental occurrence.

The basic process for all sales has not changed much. However, how that process is executed has not changed enough. The most notable paradox that developed is that, on the one hand, more information is available than ever before, on literally everything. On the other hand, the rate of change has increased to the point where there is not enough time for the buyer to learn all that is seemingly necessary so as to ensure making a sound business decision.

There is only one way out of that trap and that is for the buyer to knowingly make decisions, with imperfect knowledge, trusting the seller in the process of doing so. The seller, also faced with a time constraint albeit of a different kind and source, cannot afford a haphazard approach

front-end consulting will help.

to establishing trust and presenting product. Both parties realize they can't know for certain and know right away, simultaneously. Pick one.

4. *Developing the usable methodology is prelude to the next purpose.* The more complex task of re-orienting that business development person to the four elements (seller's company, product, market and buyer) and then, as important as anything, re-orienting them to themselves. To be effective, they need to be more than just sales people — and it starts with them adopting that greater position and posture. Of consultant. Of contributor. Of partner.

Bingo!

That involves a possible change in attitude as well as behavior. It means taking on more responsibility, being more committed, involved, open, vulnerable. Not all sales people will make the change, or even want to. That doesn't mean they will fail. It just means they will work harder then to maintain any respectable level of accomplishment.

What about a consultant changing to sales?

5. *All the required change in and to the salesperson takes time and effort.* Few people are changed by reading a book — unless they re-read and have the opportunity to put into practice what is being discussed.

After presenting the basic rationale of what's happening in the marketplace, and some of the new tools available to the salesperson (and manager), we focus attention on what anyone responsible for selling needs to know and do before they even pick up the phone, let alone make a face-to-face call. There are too many situations and variables to present all the answers. In this case, knowing the questions to ask is sufficient; the reader can supply the answers.

Because the time/place metric is totally individual and personal, no two readers will answer the questions the same way — nor need they. If the answer is to be standardized, put it in a brochure or on the Internet. Sales people are, first and foremost, people. They filter and interpret information, relating it to themselves and their client. That's the essence of Relationship Selling. If there is no need or opportunity for this personalization in the sales process, then it's incumbent on management to totally automate the sale and delivery of the product. Use an ATM, the

Web, a vending machine or a catalog. Hire marketing staff, not sales. In those cases, that *is* the end of selling.

6. *The last reason — and for some the best — is to allow business development people the opportunity to step back from their day-to-day activity and reflect on what they are doing.* Can it be done differently? Better? Should it be done at all? That kind of evaluation should be done daily or at least as each new activity is encountered. For whatever reason, that seldom happens - until there is a cause. The cause is invariably a negative of some kind, something that might have been avoided had the time been taken to do the reflection and evaluation beforehand.

Every day needs a little bit of slack built into it. If the schedule is too tight, it won't work. Think of a ball and socket that have matching dimensions so that the ball fits exactly into the socket. It binds and won't move. It needs just a bit of space and a lubricant. Personal interfaces are no different; they need a little space and something to make them move a little easier.

A business person with any responsibility, certainly anyone creating customers, needs the space and time to reflect rather than to just do. To do intelligently, with awareness, is infinitely more productive than to merely do out of duty or habit. And just as the best sports stars need a coach, a counselor, a separate set of eyes disengaged from the immediate play, so too does anyone charged with the responsibility of creating customers.

That's what good training does, by book or class. Sales people don't need training as much as feedback, from their team as well as their coach. The better they are, the more they need it and the more they look for and respond to it. Now, when the entire process is changing, anyone involved in the complex transaction will either change with it or face spending the rest of their business career walking the Santa Monica beach with a metal detector.

Chapter 2

Rules of Engagement

If the activities that collectively had been referred to as selling are now being transformed — Luddites would say transmogrified — into customer creation, with sales people becoming business development managers, then it should be no surprise that the process starts with the individual concerned, the one who never told mom what the new career was all about because mom would have suggested he get a real job. Part of that problem is the baggage that has accumulated with the title 'salesperson,' baggage as wanted as the barnacles that accumulate on a boat bottom. The majority of the problem is that the new responsibility termed customer creation requires a totally different approach, attitude and persona.

As with any paradigmatic change, some participants are already either there or well on their way, others will welcome the opportunity and challenge (and rewards) while still others will have difficulty or might have already made a down payment on a metal detector. For those individuals who have any inclination to take on this newly defined and exciting commercial responsibility — arguably the most important function of the enterprise — we offer several axioms that will pave the way.

Axioms are self-evident truths, as near universal as it comes. Hence, some of what follows may not be headline news. And we're still not playing with secular scripture and moral imperatives. The only surprise might be how well they fit and explain certain aspects of the new customer creation process.

1. *Each one of us is totally responsible for everything that happens in our life.*

Nowhere is this a more critical truth than in sales. This is not a new concept. You've heard it before, from your parents, teachers, clergy, maybe even your sales manager. What it really amounts to is your most basic choice in life. If you choose not to be responsible for your life, then you've chosen to be a victim. Many people so choose, consciously or otherwise. Victims do not make successful anything — because by definition they never lead, cause, or take the initiative. They live a life of consequence to someone else's action.

However, taking responsibility for one's self is undoubtedly easier said than done. To begin with, it's a binary decision: either you are responsible, or you're not. Moreover, either you are responsible for all of it, or none of it. You can't just take credit for the good and the great, and pass on the bad and the least. It's an all or nothing game. If you choose self-responsibility — surely the preferred route — the challenge is then to apply it consistently, on a daily basis.

However, if we each take the responsibility for our lives, then we are saying 'I am what I am because of myself.' That gives each of us the opportunity to choose what to do about it. It gives us a freedom we would not otherwise have. Freedom's not just another word for nothing left to lose; freedom is the other half of the responsibility coin. The two come as a package deal. Which ever one you take, you get the other, like it or not.

That fact alone makes self-responsibility worth-while — not necessarily easy, but very worth-while. The freedom to choose — or to choose to not choose — is one of the great gifts of humankind. To consciously choose to act — or not act — is to then take responsibility for our being what we are. It doesn't get any better than that.

As a business development person, you will rightfully receive kudos for the sales you bring in to the company. You must also take the responsibility for the ones you didn't; your losses. And not just some of them; *all* of them. That doesn't mean you have to beat up on yourself — that's not what responsibility is all about. It's a matter of accountability, determining what you will do differently next time, what you can change. Self improvement is inherent in the process; as good as you are, you'll get better. That's just one of the benefits of taking responsibility for yourself.

2. *The world that we each perceive is no more than a mirror of our own mind.*

We each, alone, create our own reality. If our mind is negative — or positive — our world will be negative — or positive. A mind full of doubt will create a world full of doubt; a mind full of beauty will create a world full of beauty.

The story is told of a family that had to relocate because of a change in the husband's employment. To learn more about the new town they were to make home, the man drove to the new town to check it out. When he arrived at the center of the town, he found an elderly fellow sitting on a park bench in front of the old courthouse.

"Excuse me", our visitor said addressing the elderly man, "I'm new here. I wonder if you could tell me something about your town?"

"Where are you from?" asked the old man. "What was that place like?"

"Oh, it's a wonderful town. Great neighbors, and a terrific school for the kids. Clean, and really friendly. We're sure going to miss it and all the great times we had there. What's this town like?"

"Well", said the old man, "I guess you'll find it just about the same as the town you're leaving."

Satisfied, our visitor returned home, pleased to know that maybe moving his family wouldn't be such a bad thing after all.

Shortly after he left his new-to-be-town, another man came upon the same old man, still sitting on the courthouse park bench. The second visitor also asked about the town. And the old man asked the same question about where he was from and what it was like.

"Well, as a matter of fact, I'll be darn glad to get out of that town. There isn't a decent teacher in any of the schools. The streets are always littered, the neighbors are lousy, even our preacher is a jerk. I can't stand the place. But what's it like here?"

"Well," said the old man, "I guess you'll find it just about the same as the town you're leaving."

If you start your day knowing it's going to be a bad day, odds are you'll be right. The contra is also true.

The challenge here is that the human animal does not naturally think in terms of Aristotelian logic. We do not normally think: if A, and if B, then C. Rather, we think: if *not* A, and if *not* B, then C isn't going to happen either. In other words, we reason negatively and in consequence we tend to think negatively. We look at our watch — to see what time it isn't. We don't look and say: it's 11:15; we say it isn't lunch time yet. Someone asks: What are you doing for dinner: And we answer: Nothing. We *are* doing something - but we answer in the negative.

The successful business development person has consciously, reoriented his speech pattern, thought process and action plan to always be positive. A positive statement, a positive cause or reason, a positive rather than a defensive action. To the extent that you are positive oriented, your audiences (prospects, clients, peer group, management) will be positive. The contra is also true.

3. *We say what we are, but we are what we do, and we do what we choose.*

> Consciously or unconsciously. Most of what we know is from second-hand information. It's what we've read or heard, but it's not first-hand experience.

That's true of ourselves and true for the people we deal with. We seldom have the opportunity to share an experience let alone a seminal event. So we accept what is said, and hope that what we say is accepted as well. But what is said and what is done might be quite different, accidentally, intentionally and even unconsciously. Sales people were seldom held responsible for doing what they said because "after all, they're trying to sell you something." But that was then and this is now and the buyer doesn't need the salesperson for information anymore.

Today's business development person *is* held to a higher standard. What is said and what is done requires congruency, and that is simply a matter of choice.

There are those who say we are not always in a position to choose — the poor, for instance, the uneducated, the handicapped. But there are too many illustrations of the disadvantaged overcoming adversity because they chose to see opportunity rather than obstacle. The greater likelihood is that we choose unconsciously, that we are not necessarily always aware of making a choice because we are not clear on our goals and responsibility.

Conscious choice will narrow any gap between what is said and what is done. Conscious choice is one of the primary differentiators between humans, all other animals, and most marigolds. It also is the primary difference between high performance people and the average.

4. *You have at your hand everything you need to resolve any situation you confront.*

> Please note — it's not that you have everything you *want* — you probably don't. But you do have everything you *need*. We've all

heard the admonition to "think outside of the box." More basically it's merely to think. It may result in an unorthodox approach to the situation, an outrageous solution, an unheard of methodology. The only important question is: does it resolve the situation you confront?

We lived in Argentina for a year and more back in their days of rampant inflation. The work contract called for being paid in US dollars but shortly after arrival we were told it was going to be take it in pesos or go home. With the peso losing five to ten percent of its value each day it was a question of how to get rid of the peso as quickly as possible. In short order, we worked out a system where as soon as we were given our peso check we ran across town to the commodities market, bought as much beef as our money could buy and shipped it to the Smithfield Market in London, sold it for British Pounds, transferred those to our New York bank and converted that to US dollars. Did we lose a little on the overall transaction? Sure, but not nearly as much as two days of inflation would have cost.

Are you part of the problem or part of the solution? That's just another one of your many daily choices. Creating customers in today's high tech market is not a matter of knowing every last detail of your product, nor is it the slickest presentation, smoothest talker, shiniest shoe. In large part it's 'Can you solve my problem?' Which means 'Do you understand my problem?' Which translates to 'Do you understand me?'

Another example: A small engineering company in the Midwest had formulated a computer software mapping system that could provide the three things that all county commissioners are concerned about: 911 emergency service, infrastructure (read: roads, bridges and culverts), and property taxes. Because of their sophisticated technology, the engineering company could provide the service at a price substantially lower than their competition. But the county commissioners didn't seem to be interested. The engineers kept talking price and savings and the commissioners kept saying, "We'll see." The conundrum was solved one day when one of the commissioners finally said: "Listen, there's an election coming up in another three months. What does this do for my campaign? Hang the cost. Am I going to be around here next year?"

That anecdote brings out the flip side of this axiom: having everything you need to resolve the situation you confront means you have to first understand what the situation is. All too often we spend an inordinate amount of time coming up with a great solution to the wrong problem.

5. *A goal remains a wish until you add a clock and a plan.*

Indeed, a wish, clock and plan is what defines a goal. There needs to be an understood, step-by-step process of getting from here to there. That means you must also have a clear understanding of where 'there' is. And at the risk of sounding simplistic, that means you must also know where 'here' is. But even given all that clarity and understanding and procedure, it won't happen until it's scheduled, until time is applied to the equation. Time alone does not make things happen; time just keeps them from happening all at once, or never happening at all.

It's often the distance between 'here' and 'there,' coupled with the unilateral dimension of time that keeps a goal from being realized. The clock keeps running, whether you have a schedule or not. All that means is that your plan must be action oriented. That step-by-step process you've laid out requires someone to do something —not just think something. To take an action is to live with that plan and schedule.

It sounds so simple — and, indeed, it is. The obvious question then is: Why don't more people set goals *and* accomplish them? It might be because many people live in a vague world where metrics are difficult to quantify.

In business development there is no lack of potential metrics — what do you want to measure? Number of sales? Dollar value? Number of calls? Number of prospects? Any good sales person, novice or experienced, hi-tech or low, male or female, sets goals. Daily. Weekly. Call-by-call. Whatever fits the situation.

Choosing what to measure is the easy part. The difficulty is in setting the measure. It's the 'how much' of metric, not the 'what.'

All metrics that measure our own performance contain an element of the most personal metric we each have: our own sense of time/place; that is, where am I now? This moment. Me. Here. Now. No one else can answer that question, for me or for you. And each person will have their very own answer — which can vary by day, situation, or even mood.

Setting a goal, then, is an extremely personal and in most cases, private, thing to do. Most discussions about setting goals concentrate on setting the big goals in our life —I want to grow up to be President, or a fireman; I want to make a million dollars by age 30, or whatever. The more successful people I've met in life set much smaller goals — but they set them several times a day, for every situation they're involved in. And it seems to work. I am reminded of a bumper sticker that read: "Never mind world peace. Try to visualize using your turn signal."

6. *You, in your multiple roles of business developer, are in a position and have the power to build people, and companies, and whole markets.*

This is a matter of vision, a question of how big is your horizon and what do you dare to dream. Start by knowing that the first statement is a fundamental truth. Others have done it before you; others will do it after. You can do it now.

Let's discuss this vision thing, your 'world view.' What's out there in your future? What are you capable of accomplishing? Is your world eight to five, no bigger than the edge of your desk and thank God I have the weekend off? Or is there more? Something you can improve, something you can contribute in addition to 8 hours of time? What can you learn so that your contribution is greater? How far are you going with this job, this company, this experience? How far do you want to go? And are you laying bricks or building a cathedral?

Practice expanding your horizon, how big you think, what you can realistically imagine. You don't have to think big to begin with; if you can't imagine yourself giving a presentation to the 100 top executives at GM, can you see yourself doing a one-on-one with the CFO of a small company? Determine your comfort level, and then stretch it. If you're comfortable running a nine-minute mile, set a target of 8:45. And when that becomes your new comfort point, re-set it to 8:30. The same holds true in business. Are you comfortable running a million-dollar territory? Increase it and take on an assistant. Comfortable managing a 200-person business development operation? Determine what you can do to contribute more. And all the while, understand that it's not how hard you work — quantity is yesterday's measure. It's quality. Measured by ROI,

ROE, market share, shareholder value, etc. Frederick Taylor was 100 years ago; the world has moved on.

If you know both quantity and quality — and the difference — then you can also see yourself building people, companies, and whole markets. By like token, perhaps you choose to *not* build. Just make that choice consciously, fully aware of what you're doing.

Now, the next three concepts are absolutely essential for creating customers. As universals, you ignore them at your peril. To understand them, to know they are always at work and affecting your environment, will greatly aid your efforts and success.

7. *The 1ˢᵗ Law of Wing Walking.*

> This dates back to early 20ᵗʰ century aviation. Wing Walking was a daredevil entertainment at county fairs across the United States shortly after Wilbur and Orville were pronounced sane in spite of their shenanigans at Kitty Hawk. The idea was to have a person do acrobatics on the wing of an airplane while the plane was in flight, to the amazement and delight of the fair crowd on the ground.

What was not necessarily evident to those bewildered beholders was that the person walking the wing had a metal bar that had been welded onto the wing and to which the wing-walker was hanging onto for dear life. The 1ˢᵗ Law of Wing Walking, then, simply says: "Never let go of something until you have a good hold of something else."

While that served as a basic rule for those fearless few, it also happens to be a truism for the way most people lead their lives (of quiet desperation, as Emerson would say). We all know people who hate their job — but stay there because they haven't found another one. We even know couples who stay married in spite of it being a dysfunctional relationship — but they haven't found an alternative yet.

What's important to realize in business development is that's the way your prospect thinks and acts. There won't be acceptance of what you're proposing until it is seen as a better alternative than what they already have. No matter what you are offering — brown shoes, treasury bonds, a vacation retreat, or a bulldozer, your prospect is already doing something in the absence of your solution. It might not be as good, new, shiny or strong as what you have to offer, but it works. It might not be much but it's better than a free-fall with a bad parachute.

Know that it is unlikely that anyone — child or adult, friend or foe — will give up a known for an unknown. Asking for that is asking for a leap of faith. The clergy ask for that and, even with eternal damnation as the alternative, their conversion rate is not all that good. The alternative you are offering must be perceived as better than what they have — or there is no chance of a transaction. It's that simple. But just because it's simple doesn't mean it's easy. How much better, and what and where better are oftentimes a matter of the client's perception. You, as leader of the band, have to figure it out. The good news is that computers can't do that. To the extent you can you won't be a part of a disappearing profession.

8. *The 2nd Law of Thermodynamics –*

was said more elegantly by someone else long ago, but what it essentially says is: "Unless you do something about it, things will get worse." It's the law of entropy, and it applies to iron bars rusting, houses getting dirty, relationships deteriorating, sales not getting done.

Note that it doesn't say 'things won't improve.' It says 'things will get worse.' Life does not stand still — it goes forward or backward but it is never motionless. You might stand still, yet the world continues to revolve under your feet, taking you with it, like it or not.

Entropy was originally a term used only in physics and chemistry — until sociologists began poking around for ways to justify their science. And the term fit. Entropy does apply to interpersonal relationships as equally as it does to rusting automobiles or the disappearance of the Roman baths in England. A relationship kept active by all parties concerned will not suffer from entropy. The 1926 Duesenberg that looks like it just rolled off the production line has been cared for, treated as a dear friend as long as it has been around. And the Roman baths weren't.

The important part of the law is the first phrase "Unless you do something about it." You *can* impact anything in your life - maybe not *every*thing, but certainly *any*thing. We're back to priority and responsibility, what's important and what's urgent.

9. The Ultimate Law of Human Behavior.

This isn't the first time you've heard this; several philosophers have said it for a long time: People will always do that which they perceive will most benefit themselves. Said another way: People will not purposefully act against their own self-interest.

To an observer it might appear that a person's action is solely for the benefit of a second party. That second party might well receive a benefit — but the greater benefit is always to the person acting. The reward is often more a moral than a monetary victory, or it's an expression of deeply hidden personal values that even the actor is not aware of having.

There is always the temptation to think that people will be motivated to act in favor of their most material gain. While that might often be true, and while it might often appear that way, it's a mistake to draw that conclusion as a universal. Certainly its an error when you're involved in a business-to-business transaction, where a person is charged with spending corporate money. Then the equation for action becomes much more complex. Survey after survey shows that price ranks no more than fourth - and often much lower — as a decision factor in the complex sale. As the business development person, your challenge is to understand enough about your client's value system to know what personal motivations are in play, what objectives and goals can be satisfied and how your product/service offering relates to it all.

An interesting example of self-benefiting action occurred on a grand scale in China, shortly after the Communists took over in 1949. Because public services such as garbage collection fell to a low during the transition in government, the major population centers experienced a significant increase in rat population.

At what seemed the height of the problem, the Chinese powers that ruled decided they could bring the rat count under control by paying a bounty to anyone bringing a dead rat to the local authorities. And in short order, thousands of rats were being turned in for the money.

Now the question is: Did this reduce the rat population? And the answer is an emphatic: No. The enterprising Chinese public saw an opportunity — rats have a short gestation period and a litter will go between eight and ten. With very little space needed for garbage as raw material, one could start a rat-farm and easily double a meager income. In fact, with an aggressive approach, one could become rat-rich. And many did.

The point is evident, if extreme: people will always take that action which they perceive to most benefit themselves, and it holds true in all corners of the commercial world, as well. For instance, sales quota and commission plans are written to the benefit of sales management. 'Sales plan lawyers' will study their commission plans and conduct their sales activity so as to benefit their own performance and income. The experienced sales manager knows this and builds it into the commission plan. Prospective clients will evaluate and discuss openly your proposal in terms of its impact and consequence to their Company — and as sure as little kids love mud, they're also thinking through how it affects their career, security, next raise or promotion, in short: what happens to me? The answer to that question is built into their support of or resistance to your proposal.

Conclusion: While the objective of selling remains the same — create a customer — the activities involved in accomplishing that have changed dramatically. How you as a business development person think and understand the world around you and the people you interact with will provide the foundation and the extent of your success.

To approach customer creation as a profession — a disciplined commercial activity that will not only provide a very satisfactory level of income but also serve as a rich, rewarding and fulfilling business career — the concepts above are fundamental. Exercise self-responsibility; know that you create your own reality; understand that what you (and others) *do* is more important than what is *said*; that everything you need you already have; that goals require action — yours; that you have the ability to change the world. Then also know that no one will change until they understand the benefit of doing so, that if you don't do something, things will get worse, and that everyone — even you — will always act in their own self-interest.

All of these work in the world of commerce. They also apply in dealing with your children, neighbors, the guy across the street. They are universal, which make the results predictable, which make your actions more effective and efficient. And as important as anything, no one has been able to program a computer to do any of it. These are the things that make the responsibility of customer creation a truly human task.

The end of selling? Quite possibly. But it's also the beginning of a better business practice.

Chapter 3

The Sales Cycle

It's probably time to abandon the title 'salesperson,' at least for the complex transaction. 'Sales' and 'salesperson,' even though politically correct, carry too much baggage, accumulated over the past few centuries. Besides, the activity has changed, as has the responsibility; the baggage, therefore, is nearer to being garbage. The term in question can be replaced with 'account representative' — but that's a bit generic and bland. Some are already using the term 'customer relationship manager' which conjures up images of an Activities Director at a retirement community. One could use variations on the theme of 'customer creation' — but that smacks of new age philosophy, with small children tossing sequins on the path leading to the first prospect call while an orchestra plays Mendelsohn in the background.

Something like 'Business Development' on the other hand, has the sound of strength and purpose while describing the activity as well as the responsibility. And whose mother would object to their child being gainfully employed in furthering the American Dream of developing business? Being a salesperson ranks along with dockworker or playing the piano in a house of ill repute; being in Business Development sounds legal, intellectually challenging and non-fattening.

Discounting, then, the Shakespearean assumption that a rose by any other name is still a rose, it might be well to define exactly what is the process of creating a customer, what and how it has changed — and what hasn't. The activity begs for definition to the benefit of all parties concerned. 'Sales' and 'selling' are terms applied indiscriminately to everything from impulse purchases to extortion which is reason enough to drop the terms and carefully define the replacement.

First, exclude most retail purchases in that they are initiated by the buyer. Also exclude what can be classed as the simple transaction — one buyer, one seller, one call, and one decision — where the objective is to sell once, grab the money and run. That's an event, not a process. That leaves the complex transaction; multiple people on both the vendor and the buyer teams, multiple calls, multiple decisions, multiple opportunities to accomplish something or nothing, and a longer elapsed time for the whole activity. For some, it might be semantics to call the process 'creating a customer' rather than 'selling.' It's really much more. It's the difference between fixing a pothole in a country road and building an Interstate highway, the difference between kissing your sister and falling in love with the girl next door.

To reduce the process to a one-sentence definition, customer/client creation is: *to cause someone to take an action they would not otherwise have taken.* That's general enough to include the simple as well as the complex transaction. It also can cover a lot of personal or non-business transactions, i.e. your child and their homework, where to go for family vacation, etc. It's not politically correct to refer to your spouse or child with a commercial term — but the analogy holds true. It also illustrates the point that we all spend a lot of our time selling something. We might not term it selling but we are creating a customer, a buyer, for our thought, idea, or world view. We are causing someone to take an action they hadn't planned to take.

Please note that the first operative word of the definition is 'cause' — not convince, force or coerce. Those terms take power and choice away from the prospective customer; cause leaves power and choice with them, along with a comfortable feeling. Note also that the activity requires the client 'to take an action.' Some might argue that changing a belief is sufficient, but belief is best demonstrated by action. Besides, we all have beliefs, many founded on commercial or social mythology which, when put to the test of action, disappear like vodka in water. The final phrase, 'would not otherwise have taken.' is also key. If the customer was going to do it anyway, the transaction would be classified as order taking, which means you didn't create a customer, they became a customer by self-proclamation. Same coin, but the other side.

Like so many other things in life, you'll know when you have created a customer. It's like knowing when you've made the perfect golf shot, when you've accomplished a personal best in a marathon. No one needs to tell you — indeed, no one else can tell you. You feel it; you know it; it's your high.

Now, having said all that, and agreeing on the definition, realize the enormity of the task. Just how does one go about causing another to take an action they would not otherwise have taken when the technology behind the solution is changing faster than the customer can absorb it, you and your competitors all have functionality that exceeds the individual

23

needs of a prospective customer, and the Internet delivers more information than even the best salesperson can remember? This is where the old school of selling falls apart, crumbles, becomes useless.

The goal remains the same — create a customer — and the basic steps to accomplish carry the traditional labels, as you'll see. But the roles and responsibilities of both seller and buyer are changed. There has been a power shift based on information availability. That affects objectives, process and alternatives. Which in turn creates more complexity which changes the roles and responsibilities of both seller and buyer, etc., etc.

The old school of sales and selling continues to preach static structure and scripted dialogue, playing a numbers game that says 200 cold calls nets 20 legitimate suspects which will result in 10 prospects, 5 calls and 1 sale. Therefore, goes the argument, to double your sales, make *400* cold calls, etc. Save that kind of logic for auditors and other unimaginative souls.

In actual fact, most selling is done by a salesperson who is given less than adequate training before being shoved out onto the street, who then tries any number of approaches. Finally one works and a sale is made — and *that* sales approach is used from that day forward. It could have been an accidental sale, a lucky break, a desperate buyer, or any number of other reasons that actually caused the transaction to take place. Nonetheless, the sales person has a win and that causes repetition in the belief that if it worked once, it will work twice. Tried often enough, it will. Beat it into a pattern of activity and it becomes a sales persons' style. And a sales manager's nightmare.

There is a better way, no more difficult than you choose to make it. It turns most of accepted sales and selling wisdom on its head, makes use of the new realities of the market-place, accepts buyers as intelligent knowledge workers, and treats the whole activity as a profession.

Some will say there's no need to change anything; the old system still works. There's just enough truth to that statement to keep it from being a falsehood. It's a bit like saying that if you don't know how to start a car, you can still get to Chicago by pushing it all the way. And, yes you could — but why would you?

The step-by-step process of creating customers, in its most fundamental form, looks pretty much as it always did:

- Create an awareness of need in the prospect's mind

- Present your product/service
- Generate a desire to have the need satisfied with your product/service
- Agree to agree on the solution
- Provide the necessary (and then some) follow through

That is as simplistic a cycle for creating a customer as can be constructed. In real life, those five steps become 10 or 50 or 100, depending on the product, the marketplace, the company providing the product/service, the client, and the person responsible for business development. Further, all of it is within the context of the larger purpose of establishing a long-lasting relationship with that client. Nonetheless, there are things to learn from examining these simple steps in the light of current realities.

Step One

To begin with, the initial step is to create an awareness of need. It is not to create the need — just the *awareness* of it. The client might or might not be aware of having a problem much less than that there is a product to solve it. All too often the client suffers from the 'forest and trees' syndrome; that is, they are so close to their daily work that they might not realize there is a better way to operate.

The business development person on the other hand has the advantage of 1) being disengaged, and, 2) seeing similar variations of the same problem in every client contact made, day in and day out. The challenge then, is to have the client verbalize his version of what the situation appears to be. At the very least, he will describe the problem as he sees it, not as your solution sees it. As a beautician once said: "People don't come into my shop saying; 'I'd like a bottle of tea-lauryl sulfate with cationic protein polypeptides, sodium citrate and some red dye #33.' They come in and say When I get out of bed in the morning my hair stands up — what should I do?"

When the prospective customer describes his problem he is also, directly or otherwise, describing his relationship to that situation and even the urgency of a needed solution, using his words and, wittingly or otherwise, expressing his feelings. How valid, direct and meaningful these are, will depend on the relationship you have with that client. The closer you are to being partners, the more valid, direct and meaningful the words are likely to be. The outcome of this process for you, the business development person, is that you can then describe your product/service in the same terms that your client just used. Or, conversely, they might have said enough to have you realize that they don't need your solution. That being the case, you can move on. Doing so is possibly the most distinguishing characteristic between the seasoned professional and the novice. The experienced senior realizes that not all the world is waiting for them with bated breath, that their fair share of the market is less than 100%. Persistence is a two-edged sword. Knowing when to 'hold them, when to fold them' is a large part of the process of success.

Additionally, most needs have an urgency factor that determines priority. The problem you're addressing might not have risen to the top of the list yet. The need is known but other things have priority for scarce resource. You might be able to increase the sense of urgency by presenting consequences — positive or negative. Then again, you might want to just come back at a later date.

The one other dimension of the situation is that each person in the decision making group invariably has a different set of needs. What touches one can be irrelevant for another. The business development person, then, has the task of recognizing the needs of each person in the group, judging their similarities, differences or possible conflicts, searching for a universal need that all can identify with and relating it all to the product/service being offered. That's putting your systems/analytical thinking skills to perfect use.

Step Two and Three

Having done all that, there comes a point where the product/service that addresses the condition must be presented. Because the client articulated the perceived need, the attentive business development person will be aware of how to describe the product/service in terms the client understands. At the same time, it's necessary to generate a desire to solve the problem with your solution. That's done by linking a benefit and consequence to every point being described, be it generic, augmented, expected or future. Any feature, function or point that does not have a benefit and consequence for the particular audience being addressed should not be mentioned. No benefit means no significance — keeping in mind that one man's frustration can be someone else's Mother.

Indeed, as with decisions, benefits come in at least two sizes (personal and corporate) and in half a dozen colors, to wit:

- Is the benefit personal or corporate, and which is likely to be more effective? This is not a matter of personal gain versus corporate loss, nor is it the reverse of that. It's a choice of two more or less equal benefits — and the smart choice would be: the personal. Just as there has never been a recorded incident of a man being shot by his wife while doing the dishes, there is no record of anyone ever choosing something against their own best interest.

- If it's a question of an emotionally based benefit vs. a rational one, of feelings as opposed to Aristotelian logic, go for the feelings. At the same time, provide a rational version that can be used with peers and others to explain the decision. No person will go to their next in command and say 'I decided to go with Charlie because he's a nice guy; he makes me feel comfortable'. That doesn't come across as a business decision. Throw in a line about cost or quality, long term ROI or dedication to emerging technology — then everyone can win.

- How about immediate benefits vs. future? short term vs. long term? In a culture that has become disappointed with a computer screen if it doesn't change within three seconds, a society that has raised immediate gratification to an art form, choose the short term over the future. It's not that people don't believe in the future; it's that the future takes too long to get here.

- When the choice is to offer a tangible benefit or an intangible, the Missouri 'show me' takes center stage. Bankers make money lending against hard assets, things they can repossess when the loan goes bad. Software, for years, got the Rodney Dangerfield treatment because you couldn't see it. Even now, the respect given software is not because of the software, but rather because people see the tangibles their neighbors have as a consequence of buying Internet stocks. There's assurance in the tire you can kick; there's truth in the house that can be foreclosed.

27

- And if the alternative is measurable versus unquantifiable, for instance a 20% increase in net profit versus the promise of a more loyal customer base, there is no need to call in Adam Smith for the decision — take the 20% profit and run.
- The last benefit choice, large versus small, is a bit trickier. The first follow-on question is: does small preclude incremental? If not, there will be that group of people who are inclined towards playing it safe and would prefer the small because the risk is also perceived to be small and there's still the opportunity for more. So the second question becomes: what's the risk threshold of the decision maker? Large versus small is a slam-dunk for large; large versus small but incremental is a balancing act, a judgment call.

In stating the benefits of a solution, then, choose the personal, emotional, immediate, tangible, measurable and large — or small and incremental — knowing that you could have gone the other way if necessary. There is no right or wrong — a benefit is a benefit. Deal with it.

An important further step is to translate the benefit into a consequence. It's the 'so what?' of the benefit. The payoff. If the benefit of buying a newer car is reliability and fewer break-downs, then the consequence is you're more likely to get to work on time and improve your performance record. If the benefit of a new software system is lower costs of operation, the consequence is increased operating margins. If the benefit of attending college is more education, the consequence is increased life-time income. Etc, etc. *w/o negative connotation*

Benefits invariably have multiple consequences — some evident, some hidden. And a consequence is subject to the same bi-polar analysis of a benefit (personal or corporate, emotional or rational, etc.). A potential trap is to assume a consequence, particularly when it's not evident. The benefit of a new car not breaking down and causing delays might not have a consequence in employment performance; he might want the girl next door to notice the new car. Better to allow the client to voice both benefit, and with your encouragement possibly being needed, the consequence. Then repeat it to make sure you're on the right track.

On the premise of there being a valid, expressed need, this iterative process of description and benefit/consequence statement should, in sports parlance, move the ball down the field. Done with skill and integrity, taking into consideration all the variables of decision-making, relationships, life-cycles, and now benefits and consequences, the offered solution to the problem takes on a desirability, a degree of urgency. It's a natural human tendency to want to take action when the positive consequence of that action becomes evident, even if only as a mental vision.

Step Four

That puts the process at the point where most other texts on selling say: "Go for the close." However, in today's marketplace of complex transaction, 'the close' is not an event, it is part of the process. It does not happen at once; it happens individual by individual among all parties involved in the decision-making chain, over time, in no particular sequence, with varying degrees of urgency and a near predictable incidence of dissention by someone at some point.

Further, 'close' implies an end. If business development is charged with creating customers, it doesn't end when a transaction takes place; it begins. The term should really be changed to *open*, or *beginning*. Closing the sale is invariably described as the seller's responsibility. In actuality, looked upon as an opening, it becomes a matter of an agreement between the several parties, both buyer and seller. It's not a "win" nor is it a "win-win." It's a "win together," with all parties benefiting.

Throughout the process of building the relationship and jointly discovering the positive potential of the solution (the total process sometimes being referred to as a commercial mating dance), both parties will undoubtedly experience a range of feelings, from doubt and question to wonder and satisfaction with several stops in between. When the final decision is made, it can indeed be termed a 'tension relieving activity'. An anxiousness builds up leading to the decision, and dissipates in the consequence.

The Last Step

The Peggy Lee question then comes to the fore: Is that all there is? And the answer can only be a resounding, 'NO.' If it were a close, it could be the end. As an opening, it's the start of something big. And bigger. One of the characteristics of the complex transaction is that it requires execution, implementation, training, on-going maintenance, etc. What in the past has been termed 'follow-through' really is nothing more than the preparation for the next step and the continuing activity of the partners as they exercise their relationship, to their mutual benefit.

So, that's the basic cycle: Create an awareness of need, provide a solution to that need; demonstrate the benefits and, if possible, the consequences of those benefits; agree to move forward; deliver the results. Through it all there is an on-going relationship, mutually beneficial, based on trust and focused on a common goal. With these basic — some would say primitive — steps as background, the task is to apply your product/service, company, and marketplace and to develop a cycle that fits your situation.

You'll undoubtedly end up with many more than five or six steps. For instance, the first "Create an Awareness of Need" starts with getting an appointment to talk to someone in the target account — and at that point you don't even know if it's the right person. From there to aware may well be five or six steps alone - or more.

 There are some basic questions to be asked that will help the process of constructing the cycle.

1. Where did the prospect come from? Did we find them or was it vice-versa?
   And how does it make a difference?
2. What can we learn about the prospect (both individual and company) before we even try to get an appointment? Do they have an Internet presence? Is an annual report available? Who are their competitors?
3. With whom in the prospect's company do we want to meet? And what would cause them to want to meet with us?
4. Exactly what is involved in getting an appointment? Should an introductory brochure or letter be sent? Can a third party reference be used?
5. What's the objective of this first meeting? Is a demo needed? Who needs to be involved?
6. How many more meetings will be necessary? What's the purpose of each and who will be involved?
7. How will you determine if they are seriously interested? What will they need to do? What will you need to do?

8. What can be done to accelerate the process? References? Testimonials? Product demonstrations?
9. How will you know when they have accepted your solution? What actions (if any) must they take — and what must you do in consequence?
10. What are the action steps for implementation? Who is responsible for exactly what?
11. How often and under what circumstances is the client contacted after the initial transaction?

This building of a sales cycle is not an easy task. It is filled with uncertainty, vagueness, and variation. If yours is a binary world-view — yes or no, black or white, this or that — you might have a difficult time developing your sales cycle. In the process of specifying all the steps, you will find it to your advantage to add the elements of time and cost, support materials, management and technical resources, and anything else that will help complete the transaction.

The most difficult thing to accept is that when you're finished with it, the next task is to build a better one, which means doing some serious damage to what you've just painstakingly accomplished.

At some point you're going to question the value of expending all this energy. Is it really worth the aggravation? That's a decision each must make on his own. Some people plan a trip and others just take off in a general direction. It will depend on what your objective is, what you want to accomplish, your world view and your value system. You alone determine the benefit of putting your foot forward, backward or off to the side.

This, however, can be said: a task, a sport, a discipline, an activity is most enjoyed and best executed when it has developed to the point where it is done with "unconscious competence." That is, you no longer have to consciously sort out the movements and procedure; it is done naturally, without thinking about them. That's not to say there is no thought going on, there is. But it's on a different, more productive level. To the extent that your customer creation cycle becomes so known to you, so ingrained, such a second natured activity, you can devote your energy to enhancing your activity, being more creative, more individualistic, more whatever is necessary to being successful. That's what makes business development the fun profession it's supposed to be.

The important thing to remember when talking about customer creation cycles is:

- they are not static, they are dynamic
- you're never finished building them, there are always refinements to be made
- their stability depends on the market, your product, the prospect, current competition, your company, and you. And that is not an exhaustive list.

Consequently, even a slight understanding of Chaos Theory will serve you well.

Chapter 4

Relationships - The Heart of the Matter

The sum consequence of what's affecting the market is the changing roles and relationships of the players — buyers and sellers, partners and competitors. The well defined responsibilities of each have been removed, reversed or renounced, with competitors one day becoming customers the next, with supplier loyalty taking on as much or more significance than customer loyalty, with sellers often choosing clients rather than the other way around.

Much of this has to do with information — its ubiquity and availability. There is no longer a lack of information, nor is it restricted by class or clock. Some would say there is too much information — and others would counter there is not enough time. The reality is that it is either or and both, depending on who you are and what you're trying to do. In any event it is a given that information affects a relationship to the point where the very term can benefit from a clearer definition.

Webster has six definitions of what relationship can mean, and Merriam probably has a few more. We speak of the relationship of the U.S. and British foreign policy, your relationship to your mother, the relationship the neighbor lady is having with the mailman — and each means something different. It can concern size, equality or inequality. Or it can have nothing to do with any of that. It can be tangible and measurable, or sometimes it's just a state of mind, an attitude, a perception.

In business circles, the country-club conversation is all about the importance of customer relationship, to the point where we have more than 50 computer software companies hawking an automated approach to handling the task. In fact, software will no more establish a business relationship than a shovel will dig a hole even if you stare at it for a good long time. Use the software to document the relationship, but know that documenting it will not, of and by itself, create or improve a relationship.

Ignoring foreign policy and sex for the moment, relationships of a commercial persuasion come in five basic forms, no one of them necessarily better than another, only different. Nonetheless, there is an order or sequence to them indicating a progressive spectrum if not a hierarchy.

It starts at one end with the category 'vendor' progresses to 'preferred vendor' then 'consultant' to 'contributor' and finally 'partner.' While some people assume there is a higher value as you move along the chain, doing so assigns a judgment that might be misleading, and unnecessary.

Vendor denotes a situation where the seller competes against many on the basis of feature/function and price, invariably initiates the selling task, and is more heavily involved with prospects than customers — more often than not it being a 100 to 1 ratio. Indeed, so much time is spent prospecting that little is left to develop a relationship with the person who ultimately becomes a customer.

Some products and markets lend themselves well to this equation. Products that are or tend to be commodities, in markets where prospective buyers are many but not necessarily identifiable as to when they're ready to buy. And many of those products require little if any after-sale follow-through for service or add-on functionality. If they do, the follow through activity is assigned to a customer support/service rep who is rewarded for his product knowledge rather than their interpersonal skills.

Preferred Vendor was created by buyers who finally realized that dealing with too many sellers resulted in a higher acquisition cost in spite of what may have been a lower unit price. So they selected certain vendors to be preferred suppliers; if anyone else wants to sell to those companies they must sell to or through the preferred vendor, thus making your competition the gatekeeper.

This equation works well with both product and services particularly when there is little differentiation, it's a buyer initiated transaction — and when you're the buyer. For the seller, a competitor has become the gatekeeper, which is something akin to your ex-spouse owning the only singles bar in town. No one consciously chooses to be a vendor rather than a preferred vendor; in effect, the client has just labeled you a second class citizen and that's not a good position to be in.

Preferred vendors are up a notch on vendors, but there's a bit more responsibility, a shift in accountability — in other words, there's a price to pay for the higher ranking. That will keep some vendors from ever wanting to be preferred — and that's OK as long as it's a conscious choice.

A *consultant* relationship is characterized by the buyer, with some prior knowledge of, or experience with, the seller, seeking advice or information from the seller. That might indicate faith, trust or respect on the part of the buyer — or it might be that there is no other source available. Or, it might be a litmus test of that seller. The one thing it seldom if ever will be is a paid assignment.

That it is free does not necessarily invalidate the importance of the request, nor does it denigrate the seeker or the sought. In fact, it is an opportunity for the seller to display an understanding of the prospect's industry and problem. In other words, it can earn points, further the relationship and advance the possibility of a sale.

It can also be abused by the buyer, particularly when they have no intention of buying, or when they are looking for information about the competition — yours or theirs. The junior salesperson will all too often jump at the chance to please the prospect without first determining the size or benefit of the obligation being undertaken. The mark of a senior is that they know when it's a ploy rather than a play.

Being a *contributor* signifies a major change in the relationship between buyer and seller. It means that the seller is held in high enough esteem by the buyer to be allowed to bring ideas — indeed, proposed solutions — to the sellers table, unsolicited; and that's the key aspect. Buyers seldom have time or need for unsolicited suggestions — General Motors management is not necessarily waiting with bated breath for people to tell them how to build automobiles anymore than Bill Gates wants the Justice Department to tell him how to run Microsoft.

To have this occur or even be possible means the seller has performed well in the eyes of the buyer, that the seller has demonstrated value and knowledge worth listening to. If, in addition, the idea or proposal involves a solution that does not involve the seller's own product — that is, where the evident benefit is the buyer's not the seller's — so much the better. That clearly places the seller in the category of *contributor.*

How do you make money suggesting solutions for other people's products? Well, real life is bigger than just your own product or service. Reverse the tables for a moment: What do you think of the person who only suggests activity or solutions that are obviously self-serving? What's your opinion of someone who will only suggest something if he/she materially benefits from the result?

The ultimate business relationship is that of *partner.* The best description of a partnership is that of two (or more) people, with a shared vision and goal, realizing that they can accomplish more together than what either (or any) can accomplish alone. That forces an interdependence between them and, rare as it is, it becomes a powerful force, one to be reckoned with.

True partnerships are rare because of what is required of each participant. To begin with, a partnership is possible only between equals, between individuals who view each other not as better or worse but as equals. It's the perception thing, and it's as much what I think of me as what I think of you. I'm not better or less than you, nor you than I.

The further conundrum is that interdependence is possible only between two or more solidly independent individuals. Anything less doesn't work. Multiplying 2.4 times 2.4 gives a greater sum than just adding the two together; multiplying ½ times ½ results in a lot less than either. The same is true of partnerships.

We've been describing the five levels of commercial relationship in a frame of reference of supplier and buyer but it should be evident that, other than vendor and preferred vendor, the other three are equally applicable to all other commercial relationships — competitors, partners, even investors and your own suppliers.

As you move through this spectrum of relationship possibilities, several things change. If you're operating at the vendor level, you'll have more competitors, more price sensitivity, feature/functions are more significant, and time to close — indeed, the whole customer creation cycle — is longer. As you approach the partner end of the spectrum, the converse of all those points is true.

The closer you are to operating as a partner, the more important are communication, loyalty and trust. There can be no pulled punches, no hidden agendas, no stories told out of school. The penalty for violation is extreme, and invariably quick; it's the Humpty Dumpty syndrome. Humpty Dumpty, you'll recall, sat on a wall, had a great fall, and all the king's horses and all the king's men couldn't put Humpty together again. Some things in life are binary — you either have them or you don't. Humpty Dumpty, trust and loyalty are among them. You either trust or you don't; do you know anyone you would term a little bit trustworthy or sort of loyal?

Also, as a partner, you'll probably need to invest more time and effort, and not necessarily on your schedule. Someone will call a meeting for Sunday afternoon and expect you to be there even if you had planned a family picnic. Or that business dinner conversation might last way past bedtime and your spouse is expected to understand. What spare time you thought you had might well be spent studying your partners' industry to better understand revenue streams, cost equations, and competitive threats.

The payoff comes in the form of the shorter customer creation cycle, fewer competitors, less quibbling on price, larger transactions etc. In short, better margins and profitability and more repeat business. It also is more rewarding, enjoyable and fulfilling. What you're doing takes on more meaning than just having a good income.

Finally, just a few fundamental points about these relationships:

1. Where you are on the relationship spectrum with any one client is pretty much determined by you, the business development person. You might not like what's required in a partnership. You might be very comfortable in the vendor role and not at all interested in taking the risk of moving even into a consultant role — much less the contributor or partner. The choice is yours.
2. It's also true that the client must accept the role you've chosen to play. They might not want to be your partner — at least until you've earned the right. So what can be done if the role you want to play is not what they want you to play? This is where you realize that a relationship is a two sided coin, a double-edged sword. First, I have to prove myself qualified for the role I've chosen. If I want to be a consultant, I must demonstrate my level of knowledge and expertise, voluntarily. If I want to be a partner, I must act as one rather than merely pursuing my own self-interest.

There will be times when, try as you might, your assumed role is rejected by the client because they don't want to play their corresponding role. You can't easily be a partner with someone who doesn't want to also be a partner. Most of us found that out in seventh grade when the then love of our life sat with someone else in the school cafeteria for lunch. Once again, it's a matter of fight or flight, and it's yours to choose.

3. Know also that relationship selling is not a matter of calling on the highest hierarchical position; its a matter of the type of relationship you have with whomever you're dealing with, be they janitor, clerk or President. It's possible to be a consultant to the President, a partner to the Operations VP, a contributor to the CIO and a vendor to the CFO. So what? What is important is the transaction, what is being accomplished, and by whom. It is only necessary that the relationships work. I don't have to love my girlfriend's brother; I just want to be on good terms with him so that I can continue my relationship with his sister. Likewise, in the commercial world, evaluate the relationship in terms of the goal to be accomplished.

4. Further, know that relationships are built on experiences, not technology. That latest sales force automation system might do wonders for your record keeping and that's all well and good. Building a relationship to the level of partner is a whole other story. In no way do I mean to denigrate sales force automation systems or customer relationship management software. Used within their intended purpose, such systems can be valuable aids to the professional business developer. These are record keeping systems, information repositories; they are not substitutes for interpersonal an/or social skills anymore than a filing cabinet replaces a telephone. Relationships, after all, only exist in the mind. It's what I think, what I believe, how I feel. It is a very human phenomenon — and it can't be automated. To the extent that it is the start of a process of creating a customer, it also contributes to the end of selling as we know it.

5. Finally and most importantly, technology, particularly information technology, is eliminating the vendor category. If the sales person's value-add consists of no more than reciting features, functions and price, that can be done less expensively and more consistently by an ATM, kiosk or on the Internet. Who needs the cost of a commissioned sales person?

And if the vendor disappears as market after market becomes commoditized, can the preferred vendor be far behind? The unmistakably clear message that should be coming through loud and clear to everyone in sales is: move up the food chain before Arthur Miller writes another play, with you as the lead character.

With all that as prologue, the challenge, most simply stated is: Wherever the relationship starts, and whatever the reason it started there, what can be done to move it to the next higher level, ultimately to a partnership and then maintain it as a partnership?

Not too surprisingly, it starts with the sales person understanding him/herself. Know your limits and comfort zone — and know if you want to stay there or exceed them. There is nothing inherently good or bad about being or not being a vendor, consultant or partner. It's your choice to make, consciously. Recognize the possible commitment and what will be required of you in time, energy and focus for each level.

The next step is understanding your client's business and industry, first in broad general terms, and then in their particular terms. What are their revenue streams, cost equations, obstacles? Who are the customers — and why? Who are the competitors and what are the differentiators? What are the metrics — how do they measure themselves?

You should know that for a banker the difference between 3 and 4 is either 25 or 33 1/3 (per cent) and it depends on if you're buying or selling. That means the 1 between 3 and 4 is larger than the 1 between 7 and 8 and if you don't understand that you shouldn't try to deal with bankers. You should know that insurance companies succeed or fail because of their investment policies and practices, because it's impossible to predict disasters. You should know if your client's business is capital or labor intensive, commodity or custom product, seasonal or balanced production, etc. You should know.

With increasing experience and exposure, you'll begin to talk in their terms, about their industry, about their business. Once you place yourself on the same side of the counter as your client, you no longer can be (or need be) adversarial. As you gain their respect, they'll share goals and objectives, challenges and opportunities. And so it goes.

It won't happen over night. It might require a defining moment or event. Your on-going responsibility is: do what you said you would do, without fail, and then a little bit more. That doesn't require infallibility; it just means no surprises; keep your client posted, informed.

Further, bring ideas and suggestions without being asked, and don't retain ownership of them. Once presented, allow your ego to step aside and the idea to be theirs. If possible, find the opportunity to solve one of their problems that doesn't involve your product.

And, at least once, do something for the client way above and beyond their expectation. It needn't require money — it certainly shouldn't in any way be considered a bribe. But it should be a personal expression of you and/or your company, unique to this client. That leaves out coffee mugs and inscribed ball point pens. Experience will tell you when the idea is right; just allow yourself to think creatively.

It's possible to accelerate the process of going from vendor to partner, indeed, even leap-frogging a level by a) knowing you can do it, and b) being attentive to the opportunity. Awareness is the key term here. Listening with all five senses; being involved and open to what is happening around you. Eliminating 'walls' and preconceived notions and conclusions. All of this requires energy — a lot of it. But the success of your clients' efforts returns more energy than you've expended, so there's a net gain.

The point of all this is to emphasize the importance of establishing and then working on a partner relationship with your customer. Selling, in the traditional understanding of that word, gives way to accomplishment. More gets done with less effort. Anything adversarial is eliminated. Even competition takes on a new perspective once you are on the same side of the counter as your client.

It's your choice — but then, you know that.

Chapter 5

Decisions, decisions

One can view the task of creating a customer from a number of quite different angles. It can be looked at as challenging, difficult, hard work, fun, an ever-changing experiment, an interesting experience, or even a game. From another angle, it is no more than an endless series of choices, each with their own set of trade-offs. Choice implies that decisions are being made, not only by the business developer but by the client as well and, carrying it to the next level, the decisions being made by the client are being caused by that business developer.

If your responsibility is to create customers for your company, your biggest challenge, arguably, is to cause them to make a decision favorable to your cause. Just for a moment, consider the enormity of that task. While 99% of the business populace profess decisiveness, they also claim to be risk takers, goal-driven, and to all be above average in common sense (thus creating an as yet un-named new branch of mathematics). In fact, making a decision is an un-natural act. By their very nature, humans are indecisive and risk-averse as well as being wish, not goal, driven. A doctor separates us from our disease, a dentist separates us from a failing tooth and a lawyer from our money. Your chosen task is to separate your client from their indecision, by far the most difficult separation of all.

It could well be that the excess amount of common sense that people feel they possess accounts for their indecisiveness. After all, making a decision has enough drawbacks to cause people to wonder why anyone would or should. There are few better ways to gain visibility than to make a decision. And you could be wrong. If not you, then someone you know has stood up at the curtain call of what they felt was a particularly good performance, only to find they were the only one standing. Does one continue to stand in defiance of the audiences' seeming lack of good taste, quietly sit down relieved that the majority of the remaining audience saw only your back, or spend the rest of the evening explaining to your companions that you were only preparing to put on your coat?

Additionally, making a decision opens you to outright criticism or, worse, silence. Would that the world was other than bi-polar, but for the most part, it is. Any decision is judged as good or bad, right or wrong, too much or too little, and in consequence we feel the need to choose sides. Some might take to disliking you, making life unpleasant. In all likelihood, you'll be held responsible for having made the decision, and with that, for some unknown reason, comes the self-imposed need to justify it. All because you chose.

On the other hand, the consequence of indecision is at least two-fold. First, it's quite comfortable. There's no visibility, no danger, no exposure. Second, it gives one something to do, further study the problem, take a survey, question the premise. We all know people who have made a career out of something that a decision would have brought to an abrupt end early on. Additionally, there are people — other than academics and bureaucrats whose job descriptions include indecisiveness as an attribute if not a goal — who are able to posture themselves as deep-thinkers when in reality their only contribution was to not choose.

It's fair to conclude that the odds of you causing someone to make a decision in your favor, are stacked against you to the point of making Las Vegas look like a church bingo game by comparison. All the more reason, then, to understand your challenge to beat the odds. That means you need to understand decisions and decision-making.

Just because the Internet has us awash with information doesn't mean decision-making has become any easier. Don't confuse quantity with clarity. Decision-making with perfect knowledge is an open-book exam; by definition, that's not today's business world. Managers are faced with making decisions when they not only are missing some of the necessary information, they don't even have the time to understand the information that *is* available.

Nor do they have the time to understand the professional bias and prejudice of their information sources. For instance, in the summer of 1999, Wall Street encouraged the investing public to pour money into start up firms with stock prices that were multiples of their zip codes. A year later, after the Internet stock market collapsed, those same brokers/analysts had apparently been visited by the ghosts of both Graham and Dodd — with rare exception they had all become value investors. Was Wall Street right on both counts? Wrong on one but not on the other? And if so, which one? In most cases the answer depends on whether one made money or lost it.

To begin with then, recognize that not all decisions are equal. Decision complexity can be measured by 1) the count, rank and serial number of people involved; 2) the time frame to consequence; 3) the number of variables (other than the people); 4) the quantity, quality and availability of pertinent information; 5) the perceived risk; and most importantly, 6) the alternatives and their consequences.

Now build a matrix by recognizing that any decision can be:

a) revocable or irrevocable
b) binary or incremental
c) voluntary or involuntary
d) formal or informal
e) individualized or package deal
f) precedential or non-precedential
g) individual or group or committee

And sometimes a decision involves multiple dimensions.

Examine some examples. A *revocable* decision is selecting a channel on your television. If you don't like it, you can change it with little consequence. That is, unless the viewing audience consists of more than you. The more people in the room, the more likely someone will disagree, unless the program is about to change anyhow, or they don't know what other choices they have, or they don't really care what they watch. Also, as is true of many decisions, selecting that TV channel is probably voluntary, informal, individual and non-precedential as well as revocable. It is, therefore, multi-dimensional.

An *irrevocable* decision is the first time you lie to your Mother, break a vow or violate a trust. If it's your Mother, spouse or the person who signs your check, the count is low, but the rank is higher and the serial number is one and only. Once done there's no undo icon, and that makes irrevocable decisions infinitely more difficult than the revocable, little-or-no-consequence act. Therefore, asking someone else to make the irrevocable decision requires you to be a high-priest, a world-champion, or a dreamer. In pool it's called a low-percentage shot; in business development, it's something to be avoided.

One might think a *binary* decision, a simple yes or no, would be easier than an *incremental* move. But there's more riding on the binary choice whereas the incremental suffers a smaller consequence, beneficial or otherwise. A difference between a binary and an incremental decision is

43

the difference between cliff-diving and putting your toe in the tide. Not all binaries are irrevocable but it's always the whole enchilada or nothing. Like the man said, a big mistake in life is determining to jump a chasm in two steps. Incrementally, I can take the next step into the tide, or out. The incremental decision has a shorter time frame to consequence, fewer variables, less need for information because the perceived risk and the consequence is less. It also allows the decision-making process to be continuously reviewed. Binary decisions, on the other hand, favor a negative response — the status quo is invariably a safer bet.

An *involuntary* decision sounds like a contradiction of terms but it's no more than the flip side of what we think we usually are doing; that is, making voluntary decisions. A decision becomes involuntary when it is based on something outside of the issue at hand. That could be family tradition, childhood training, a personal code of ethics or a value system. That personal frame of reference might be at total odds with the facts and evidence of the situation being discussed but it takes on the strength of law. Choosing a profession, or where and how to live, for many people is an automatic, voluntary — or involuntary — decision based on other people's expectations, prior personal experiences, religious training or a raft of other factors that have little to do with the question at hand — but nonetheless will determine the decision being made.

Likewise, there are business questions answered by a person's threshold for risk, rules their grandfather taught them on how business is conducted, and other myths by which we lead our lives.

A decision becomes *formal* when the criteria for making that decision are dictated or the environment is structured, both before and/or after the decision has been made. This sounds like a court of law — which it may be — but it can just as easily be in a commercial enterprise or a family setting. It's a matter of the players taking themselves very seriously, with rules, protocols, process and procedure. That's how some organizations, social groups and families choose to operate, with a procedure for presenting evidence or withholding it, and certain individuals by dint of title or tenure being given the right to have the last word. The *informal* is friendlier, less rigorous, and involves participants who likely realize that success is never final, and failure is seldom fatal. After all, recognized early, almost all mistakes are correctable.

A cafeteria plan is a good example of *individualized* decision making, a sheer matter of pick and choose. Whatever is on your tray when you get to the cashier is what you pay for - no more, no less. On the other hand, voting in the democratic system and marriage are examples of *the packaged deal.* You don't get part of the candidate for public office and try as you might, you don't just get the good parts of a spouse. It's an all or nothing game. In business it's very often possible, and usually desirable, to take what appears to be a package deal and restructure it to be a cafeteria offering. By doing so, choice passes to the client, minimizing risk, increasing comfort level and probably reducing time to decision.

Precedential decisions are invariably made in a court of law, according to policy and procedure. "When this happens, we do that; when that happens we do the other." It's when there are no precedents, nothing in the way of examples or guidelines, that we make *non-precedential* decisions. It's cutting new ground, going in uncharted water, investing in Internet stocks. There's less information and usually more risk because of the unknown, and quite often more alternatives than we ever thought possible.

Individual decisions would appear to be easier than *group or committee* decisions, and sometimes they are. The group decision will involve group dynamics – Who's the leader? Is there a leader? How is consensus reached? What happens to those that dissent? etc. All of that complicates the group decision. More people involved means more variables, information, and time. That changes the odds and extends the time to decision. But the individual decision forces visibility and not everyone is necessarily comfortable with that either.

Add to all of the above the growing phenomena of the knowledge worker versus the hierarchical, command and control authority that still exists in many business environments. Knowledge workers are defined as employees who by dint of their work, undoubtedly know more than their superiors, at least about the work they are doing. Many if not all hi-tech jobs bear this characteristic and it complicates any decision-making process because it has the inherent seed of potential conflict.

As the person charged with the responsibility of creating customers, you have the wonderful power to simplify the decision if not the decision-making process of your client. Given the choice, keep the decision revocable, incremental, voluntary, informal and individualized. Know that the more people and variables that are involved, the more time-consuming the decision-making process. Information quantity and quality is, or should be, a two-way street; both you and the client have an information responsibility and you'll receive more and better information as you move up the relationship ladder.

One might conclude from all of the above that causing a client to make a favorable decision is no more difficult than following a formulaic procedure. Correctly played, the game of customer creation has no losers, so where's the problem? Why aren't all decisions not only easy but positive?

Well, start with a basic truism: It's not possible to know everything and to know it now. To know everything will require time — probably more than what is allowable if action is required. Consequently, we are asked to act on imperfect knowledge and the question becomes: how imperfect can it be and still be a rational act? Can I trust the source of the little information I do have?

And that forces the all important consideration: what are the consequences *to me* if I'm wrong? We mentioned in Chapter 2 that people will not knowingly act against their own best interests; that truism, coupled with a risk threshold, will determine if a decision is positive, negative or just on hold. Many negative decisions are, in reality, merely time-dependent responses saying: "Not now." It's a matter of not having enough information to make the positive decision and knowing that most negative decisions still carry the option to be revisited at a later date.

The last thing you want to do is to ask the decision-maker why they made the decision they made. That's asking for justification, for rationality, and the odds for getting it are somewhere between 'not likely' and 'Who died and left you in charge?' The only people who want to be asked the why of their decision are those with a storybook answer, usually ego-satisfying to the story-teller and seldom of any situational value to the questioner.

Today's fast-paced business world has exacerbated the decision-making process in most organizations, changing the risk/reward ratio significantly. Time was when a promised incremental cost or profit improvement of 15 - 20% was sufficient to cause a positive decision. Now it seems the risk requires a two, three, or four times multiple to cause action. In many instances, this is merely a lack of information, and that might be really a lack of time.

Information, time and personal risk are the three legs that support the tyranny of the either/or. As the person charged with creating a customer for your organization, your task is to minimize your client's perceived risk and maximize the available pertinent information all within a time frame that most benefits all parties concerned. That can't be done with yesterday's selling practices. You need a new approach.

Chapter 6

Systems versus Analytical Thinking

Success, in almost every endeavor, is a matter of thinking, thought process, mind set. That's the principle message presented in this book because it is so overwhelmingly true of the process for creating customers. Focus is a mental process. Concentration is a mind game. Problem solving is a thinking person's pastime. Whether we are playing tennis or relating to a client in a business environment, success is more likely to the extent we are mentally at the top of our game.

This next subject, systems versus analytical thinking, is not new — but it has not been presented as integral to the process of creating customers. It is. It is a fundamental tool for anyone in business development and, just as it's difficult to win at tennis using only one stroke, in business it's necessary to think analytically and then switch to systems thinking — or anything in between — as the occasion requires. One process does not fit all situations; flexibility is paramount.

As was said earlier, we live, like it or not, in a bi-polar world. It's either this or that, things are black or white, big or small, important or trivial. People are male or female, fat or skinny, here or there. And the two different ways to look at and think about our world are: with a systems view or analytically. That is, it can be viewed as a whole, as a complete system, as the sum of all, or it can be examined in its detail, in its individual component part by part.

(For some, bi-polarity takes the form of black, or not; big, or not; skinny, or not; etc. That's no longer bi-polar — that's a single focus with exclusion for anything that doesn't fit. That thought process is at the least limiting and at the most self-destructive. Practiced in a business development role it will practically guarantee a lack of success.)

The difference between systems thinking and analytical thinking is the difference between a telescope and a microscope, astronomy and quantum physics, the animal kingdom and a fruit fly, the study of philosophy and omphaloskepsis. For the business person, primarily the business development person, both systems and analytical thinking are not only valid, both are essential to understanding what's going on.

Here's why. By definition, the complex business transaction involves multiple encounters of multiple people on both sides of the counter over an extended period of time. Each of those several people represents a separate discipline, department, responsibility, facet or interest within the corporate whole, as well as their own personal view. Using systems terminology, each person, department or functional area can be called a system, or sub-system to a larger system, which in turn eventually becomes that corporate whole. (Which operates within an industry, within an economy, within etc.)

The complexity of the transaction comes not from the nested structure of sub-system/system/corporate whole — that's both predictable and orderly. Rather, it comes because each participating individual, on both sides of that counter, is part of a decision-making process the result of which can affect their relative position within their department, as well as that department's relative position within their division and the corporate whole. And that decision-making process is anything but predictable and orderly. Is it any wonder, then, that it's called a complex transaction and that you should use as many different ways as possible to look at the situation?

The key to successfully navigating any situation is understanding the difference between systems and analytical thinking, and knowing when and how to use each. A system in this discussion can be a mechanical system (a car, vacuum cleaner, drill press), an information system (accounts receivable, payroll, inventory, ERP), a social system (a neighborhood, church group, the local pub), even a personal system (a circulatory system, nervous system, gall bladder, etc.) It starts with dependence, independence, and interdependence as applied to any part of a system, sub-system, sub-sub-system, etc.; in other words, the relationship of the parts to each other plus their relationship to the larger system they are part of, etc. It's a matter of looking at the corporate whole (systems thinking) or one person in the Shipping Department (analytical thinking); a church congregation or the Monday evening bingo game; a person's total business career or what they did at last Saturday's company picnic.

What is important to realize is that while parts, subsystems, systems and the whole have varying degrees of dependence, independence and interdependence, the underlying fact is that there is a relationship, indeed, there is an interdependence of *all* systems. That's the basis of Chaos

Theory, quantum physics, the environmental movement and most religions of the world. Yet, to believe that, to accept it as a truth, runs counter to what we are taught in our Western Christian-Judaic culture. Our emphasis is on the importance of the individual, commitment to self, the worship of the singular accomplishment. No fault is to be found with any of that other than if it is taught to the exclusion of the interdependence that is always present although not necessarily evident.

Let's use the Indy 500 Race as an example. No one will argue that to win that race is an awesome individual accomplishment. That driver — male or female, new or seasoned, shiny or tarnished — deserves every bit of the applause given. However, that driver could not possibly have won without a Cracker Jack pit crew servicing both driver and car. When 500-mile races are won by fractions of a minute, a pit stop of more than 18 seconds cannot be tolerated. That the car can be refueled and four tires changed all in less than the 18 seconds is because that crew operates as a team — each with a specific job to do, each with a carefully honed skill yet operating in concert with all other members, and the driver.

It doesn't end there. After all, there are 32 other drivers at the start of the Indy 500, each with the same goal, executing at speeds in excess of 200 miles an hour with less than 12 inches sometimes separating their vehicles. Each driver, independently, has a dependency and an interdependency with all the other drivers on the track. There are things a driver can do, and there are things they cannot do, according to written and/or unwritten rules. There's more than courtesy at stake when 33 cars are doing 250 miles per hour on the backstretch.

Likewise, there is protocol and relationship between the several pit crews, the owners and the sponsors. So it isn't just one person singularly accomplishing the fastest record of covering 200 laps. It's several hundred individuals, acting interdependently, and it doesn't end there.

Each year there are some 200,000 fans that attend practice laps and time trials. Another 400,000 go to the Race. And there's need for several thousand ushers, attendants, guards, maintenance crews and refreshment vendors. There wouldn't be a race if there were no fans, and the infrastructure is needed to handle those fans. It's all part of a system called the Indy 500. And it needn't end there because the 500 is just one of several races that constitute the circuit, etc.

That model holds true for any and all systems. As a person responsible for creating customers by introducing a new system into an existing environment, part of your task is to become totally aware of how your product/service fits into its larger system, how it interfaces, what it replaces, how it affects other systems or parts — in short, the amount of violence and dis-equilibrium you are causing. Not everyone will view your work as violent or disruptive — but others will. Some will undoubtedly look upon your work as harmonizing and personally beneficial — others won't. Basic to your understanding these several disparate reactions is your ability to apply systems and analytical thinking, to the situation and to the business development process. Systems thinking provides the big picture, the whole system, the long term view and it can lead to innovation, new concepts, different conclusions. Analytical thinking is a study of the subsystems, the parts and details; it's concerned with the short term and is directed at perfection of what is here and now. Systems thinking looks at the global warming issue and considers all temperature and weather data on a 200-year spectrum. Analytical thinking looks at the same issue by recording the high reading of a thermometer yesterday in Peoria. Systems thinking is expansionist; analytical is reductionist.

Neither form is best or preferred; both are necessary. Focus must be on the balance of the whole rather than on any one part. A juggler does not focus on one ball but rather on the whole scene. A star basketball player takes in the whole court, not just the ball. As Wayne Gretsky's famed quote points out: look where the puck is going to be, not where it is. Any focus on a part is only for the benefit of the whole. When the transmission on your car goes out, you get it repaired. In other words, you pay attention to it. Normally, you don't even know it's there. When your finger is broken it impairs the use of your hand, so you do something about it — and you're conscious of that finger until it's healed. At that point it once again loses its' visibility in your mind.

The concept of interdependence carries with it a more complex view of cause and effect than what most of us are accustomed to. If any one part was dependent only on one other part, which in turn was dependent only on one other part, etc., then it might be possible to have only one cause when something breaks down. But the world is not built on a linear relationship. By definition, if all things are interrelated, then the probability of a single cause of any situation or condition is as impossible as a kitchen with one cockroach. The search for the single cause — or even the most probable cause becomes the all too usual exercise in finger pointing. Rather than looking for the dysfunctional, look for the commitment. Don't ask "What went wrong?" Ask: "What does it take to make it right?" The time saved can be the difference between success and failure.

What is true of cause is also true of effect. Just as there are always multiple causes, any change in a complex system will have multiple effects. It isn't one thing that will result — it's several, and each to a different extent. Would that life had the stability of a three-legged stool. It doesn't. An ability to exercise systems and analytical thinking will go a long way towards being able to deal with it.

Further, understand that while the part, or sub-system, must function to fulfill its purpose, of and by itself it has no value.. It's purpose and value are determined by what it is a part of. For instance, a fuel-injection system for a Mercedes Benz 500SL, spread out on a table top by itself would be just so much carefully shaped metal and, to most people, unidentifiable. Few, if any, would be able to determine price or value. Once identified for what it is, and knowing that the car as a whole has a value in excess of $100,000, it is possible to put a value on the carefully shaped metal on the table top.

Likewise, as many in the Information Technology industry have discovered, taking the "best-of-breed" applications and putting them all together requires more time and expense than buying one integrated system even if it then requires adding additional features. If one took the "best-of-breed" — the best engine, best drive train, best suspension system, etc. — from all the automobiles produced, you wouldn't have the best automobile. You'd merely have a bunch of parts that, at best, had junk value.

It goes without saying, then, that the whole is, quantitatively and qualitatively, greater than the sum of its parts. The person charged with customer creation must have a clear picture of where and how their product/service fits into the whole system because then and then alone will they know the relative value and importance of what they are providing. To the extent that what is being provided contributes to a synergistic result, its value increases over what it is as a stand-alone item. That also allows the business development person to talk consequences rather than benefits — all of which can elevate the relationship, bringing it closer to partnership and all the good that that carries with it.

Given an involvement in a complex transaction, it is difficult to imagine anyone being successful if they are not engaging in systems/analytical thinking. Some of it, admittedly, looks like no more than common sense. It is that, but it's also much more. Tennis is more than knowing how to hold a racquet and memorizing the rule book. Poker is more than knowing how to play the cards you've been dealt — the rule book alone won't make you a winner. And so it is with systems/analytical thinking in the game of creating clients. It's knowing when to use one or the other, what to do (if anything) about the multiple causes and how to cope with the several effects, to what extent is independence essential or dependency necessary.

Now, let's go back to the basics. If the rate of technology change is exceeding the client's learning curve, applying systems and analytical thinking — that is, alternating between examining the detail and understanding the whole — will aid the business development person in communicating with the client, as well as getting a clearer picture of the situation for themselves.

A somewhat trite but nonetheless appropriate story related by one of my Harvard marketing professors years ago told of the young man who got a job in a fish market. On his first day, he asked the market owner what he should do and was told to into the back room and 'look at the fish.' Which he did.

After 10 or 15 minutes he came out of the back room, said something about a fish is a fish is a fish and asked what was next. The proprietor took a deep breath and said again, 'Look at the fish.' Sensing he missed something the first time, the lad went back and this time didn't come out for an hour. When he did, he was told to go back and look some more. After a bit, it began to dawn on the young man that there was a larger purpose being accomplished. Poking and probing, flipping and flopping, he learned more about fish than he ever imagined. There are two basic classes of fish, four different shapes, and then they can be differentiated by color, number and shape of fins, shape of the mouth, presence of teeth, thickness of skin, presence of spines, etc., etc. into any of the 30,000 species known to man. Some fish are fresh, some are fresher; if you know what you're looking at, you can tell the difference.

By the time he was allowed behind the counter, our young man knew enough to be helpful. He wasn't just selling fish; he was designing someone's dinner.

And if client expectations are exceeded by the feature functionality of the products they have to choose from, how better to differentiate your offering than by your thorough understanding of both its detail as well as how it fits into the greater scheme of things?

These are processes that won't be easily automated, and they involve interpersonal skill sets that are not necessarily familiar to many business development people. However, success in today's marketplace requires it all.

As was mentioned in the discussion on relationships, being a partner requires two complete, independent individuals to willingly engage in an interdependent effort. That partnership then exceeds the win-lose, win only and even the win-win equation. It rises to the win-together level where what is accomplished could not have been achieved by any of the parties individually.

That's the best of all results, and all that is required is a shared vision, a common goal, and mutual trust.

Chapter 7

More Cycles

Time, until someone invents something better, is the basic metric by which we measure what we do in our life. Be it getting a college degree, earning our first million dollars, or mowing the lawn, we measure by how long it takes. So too in commerce we speak of business cycles, product life cycles, and what has been referred to as sales cycles.

A sales cycle was supposed to be what happens, step by step, from point of contact to point of contract — the process of selling a specific product or service. That definition changes, expands, when our focus moves from selling something to creating a customer. The sales cycle for a simple transaction, sold by a human being or an automated device, will remain the same in scope if not in process. It's still from point of contact to point of contract (or purchase). Creating a customer will still start with point of first contact — but it doesn't end at point of contract — unless you choose it to end.

The cycle of creating a customer is larger and more inclusive than what was ever envisioned in a sales cycle, and a previous chapter developed the scope and methodology of it. Before we go too much farther, however, we need to examine some things that can dramatically affect the process of customer creation. The following chapter is aimed more at management — product, marketing, financial, general — than at anyone in business development. It concerns all things that should be considered *before* there are feet on the street.

To think that the customer creation cycle involves only those things that happen after point of contact is to see a flower garden in black and white. True enough, the cycle is shaped by the product or service in question, but also by the company providing it, the marketplace into which it is being sold, the specific buyer in that marketplace, and last but not least, the person charged with the responsibility of creating the customer.

The Product

Start with the product/service itself. Its design, architecture, structure, and package will have an immense impact on how long it takes anyone to buy it. Is it modular? Can one buy part of it and add feature/functionality incrementally? Will it require or cause violence to its environment? How much training is required to install it? To use it? Is there a talent pool of people who know how to use it or must we train all new staff?

To the extent that the required decision to purchase is binary, irrevocable and/or huge, the cycle time will be extended. Price alone will not extend the cycle but rather, will qualify or eliminate the prospect. And any time you ask a person to make a sharp left hand turn in their career path, the cycle will be extended. Such is the case when the product is in a new category or class, or if it is deemed unique. Unique products have unique audiences; they are small, narrow and not necessarily well funded. And without money, that unique audience lacks clout — or maybe it's the other way around.

What is important to realize here is that most of these factors are totally controllable. Design, architecture, required support, price and packaging — all are rightly the province of product management. There are only two product-related factors that are beyond control. The first is the economics of the sale. That is, how will the purchase of the product/service be justified economically? Return on investment? Shorter production cycles? Lower inventory levels? Cost savings? To some extent this can be affected by price, price structure and the marketing message. But by and large, it's a matter of feature/function - what does it do? What does it eliminate? What does it cause?

How a product is positioned in the market certainly is controllable. For instance Coca-Cola can be the pause that refreshes or it can be a corrosion solvent. The two uses are understandably separate with limited opportunity for cross-over advertising and promotion. But once the selling company chooses one use over the other, the economics of the sale is out of their control.

The second uncontrollable factor is the position of the product on its own life cycle. That's not to say a product life cycle can't be extended, or modified by product enhancements. Formula modifications and line-extensions can significantly affect a cycle — but the fact remains that a new product is a new product and the converse is equally true. Packaging, additives, pricing and a plethora of perception-altering marketing ploys will not change the fact that the sales cycle for a new product will be different than that of a mature product.

And now, here comes the Internet juggernaut, without destructive intent but with structure-altering consequence. If the product in question is a commodity, the Internet will mean the end of selling as we know it. The emphasis transfers to marketing, customer support and service, because the buyer knows features and function as much as the would-be sales person, including factory cost, wholesale price and mark up.

It is the readily available product information that has changed the role of both buyer and seller. It also causes the commoditization of the product. Who would have ever thought of a $20,000 or $30,000 automobile as a commodity? Yet, there's enough definition and information available on most any car to cause it to be a commodity. (Plus, we don't understand automotive engineering anymore so we buy style and price.) And there are scores, yea, hundreds of other items that have gone from complicated sales cycle to commodity, eliminating the need for a sales person in the process.

That's not to say that a person is not involved in handling the transaction; it's just not a sales person. Call it customer service, a distribution representative, or engineer, whatever. But it ain't sales. There is still a step-by-step process for moving the product off the shelf and into the customers' arms. The steps will integrate information technology with marketing, distribution, customer service and then back to the IT department and marketing for follow-up.

Even products that are not commodities can have their cycle impacted by the Internet, some more so than others. It's a fair prediction that, sooner rather than later, all products will be impacted by the new communication medium.

The Company

The company offering the product/service — quite apart from the product itself — will directly affect the customer creation cycle for the product in question. Arguably, the existing market presence of the offering company is the most important determinant of a customer creation cycle. IBM or Microsoft can merely announce an intention and begin taking orders, whereas a start-up operation must first justify its corporate existence before it can demonstrate product viability and get shelf space.

The required market presence need not be as pronounced as the example cited, but there is a required critical mass, determined by market size and structure as much as anything. The larger the market, the larger the required critical mass. The smaller and more incestuous the target market, the smaller the required mass. The relative importance of size to incestuousness is open to debate.

The marketing prowess of the company (a skill not necessarily related to its size) can also shorten the cycle. Prowess seems to be a province of the smaller firm, in part because they invariably are more nimble, have less to lose by trying something different and benefit from the publics' usually favorable disposition toward the underdog. It's also true that once the point of critical mass is achieved, the sheer bulk of market presence can replace the need for prowess. A bull in a china shop will be noticed; in a herd of a thousand, he'd have to learn to dance.

Allocated budget has an affect on more than just the morale of the marketing department. Throwing money at the problem won't necessarily solve it, but insufficient funding will create a longer than necessary cycle. The real question is not how much money is made available, but rather how should it be spent. Is it to be a marketing dollar or a commission dollar? Advertising or dealer discounts? Packaging or tailored support? The list goes on and on. But that's why CEOs earn their salary.

Having established partnerships with other vendors so as to gain quicker access to qualified prospects will reduce the lead time to proposal. It won't win the sale but it usually aids in establishing market presence. And it shortens the cycle - which means it reduces the cost, which improves the margins to increase the ad budget, which increases market awareness, etc. etc.

The structure and approach of the field force — one-on-one or a team effort; use of telemarketing as a pre-sales activity to qualify; the degree of technical knowledge required of the business developer. All can bear on the amount of time it takes for a prospect to become a client. Whatever the structure is, it will need to change as the product (or market) matures. Much of the structure also depends on the nature of the product and to whom it is being sold. Of the two, audience is more the determinant than product. After all, any product can be considered highly technical by an unsophisticated audience.

Basic to all of the above is the type of management and management process applied to the marketing and business development function. In all too many cases, the company was formed by a technician, skilled and knowledgeable in the product/service being produced but a novice at how to get it into the market — sometimes even disdainful of the role marketing and business development can play in making the business a success. The our-product-is-so-good-people-will-stand-in-line-to-buy-it school is still alive and well in today's business world.

If management participates properly in the marketing and customer creation activity, gives it a high priority for budget and attention, realizes that, in the end, all business is show business, then the cycle will be favorably impacted. The converse is also undeniably and unfortunately true.

Other than the element of market presence, all the items lumped under company are controllable. Market presence is the result of all the things that the company does or has done; in that sense it could be considered controllable, too. But for purposes of planning or analyzing a business development cycle, market presence becomes a given — it either is or isn't at that point in time and must be dealt with as such.

The Market

The third determinant is the market into which the product is being sold. The definition of what constitutes a market is a choice made by management; once the decision is made the characteristics of that chosen market are beyond control.

For instance, the chosen market could be the banking industry. Or it could be banks with more than $500 million in assets, or more than $2 billion in assets. Each choice has its own demographics, its own psychographics, a different marketing and business development equation. And consequently, a different cycle. But the seller has no control over the characteristics.

Pick whatever industry you want; it has its own numbers; it can be quantified; and it becomes a given. Big is not always better. The smaller the niche, the more easily its characteristics can be defined and identified. But the smaller the market, the less forgiving it is. Particularly is this true if small refers to geography rather than number of units. To some degree, today's communications technology renders geography unimportant —

but that's not altogether true, again, depending on the product. If, indeed, the world is your oyster, travel, communication modes, customs, life styles and tastes will differ and all will impact the customer creation cycle.

Once again, when defining a market, it's necessary to examine the impact of the Internet — the phenomenon that made global marketing what it is. The challenge is to apply the concept to your product and situation successfully, a task easier mumbled than implemented. Just because your marketing message can be sent and received around the world does not mean geography has disappeared, or that you have the infrastructure and cost equation to serve the globe profitably.

It does mean that how you formulate, evaluate and execute your sales strategy will cause the end of selling as we know it. At the least, it should cause a major change in your process because the Internet gives you a whole new dimension to work with and even if you don't use it, your competitors will.

Competition is also defined by market — and this again is chosen but once chosen becomes a given and is beyond your control. Dollar General competes with Wal-Mart not Nieman Marcus, but Dollar General doesn't tell Sam's staff what to do. Each firm has its own sandbox, and David Ogilvy was right when he pointed out that, given the same product and the same target market, any two companies will have different results because they each have different management, cultures, objectives, perceptions and abilities.

The Buyer

Not the least of the five major determinants of a business development cycle is the buyer of the product. Geoffrey Moore, in his book *Crossing the Chasm,* does a wonderful job of describing the life cycle of the product, segmenting the buyers into their five nearly discreet groups, each with distinct buying habits.

But the real world is not built that way. The fact of the matter — for the salesperson — is that all kinds of prospects express initial interest in a new product. Some because they know it's new; others because they don't know it's new. Nor are the five segments of the product cycle (innovators, early adopters, early majority, late majority, and laggards) neatly grouped out in the marketplace with all the innovators living in one town and the early adopters in another. The situation is reminiscent of a medical textbook that pictures the heart in one color, lungs in another, and the lymph system as a third. In real life, they're all together in one big mess. No labels. No evident beginning or end.

And that's what a mass audience of buyers looks like. They don't fit into neat categories, each easily distinguishable, one from the next. Furthermore, a person may be an innovator when it comes to buying sports gear for her kids and a laggard when it comes to buying clothes for herself. Therefore, labels are not only not evident, they're not possible — except for details.

Does that mean that those five categories of buyers are not valid or important? Not at all; they are extremely important. But simple, and simple does not mean easy.

Salespeople are usually taught to prospect by looking for the pain. Who is suffering because they lack your product or service? Today's business development person will be farther ahead looking for the opportunity because in many cases, the prospect doesn't feel any pain — they literally don't know what they're missing because they don't understand the new technology that is available.

The next question of do they have the money and authority to fix the pain must be expanded to include do they have the vision to embrace the new potential. It's at that point that you determine if you're talking to an innovator, early adopter, laggard, or whatever.

It's also the point where marketing and business development part company. Marketing is dealing with concepts, groups and large messages. Sales is a one-on-one game dealing with a specific situation, an individual, and an opportunity. Because the marketing department is aiming at early adopters doesn't mean your late majority buyer can't buy. It just means you have to know how to dance to a different song. The cycle will be different for each of those five categories. Not only are the message and benefits different, the step-by-step process changes — even to the point where the late majority for some product no longer requires sales people. Again, the end of selling, the start of a new kind of relationship, a better way to create a customer.

What is important to realize is that the product, company, market and buyer each have a cycle. Those cycles intersect, exist, and overlap, sometimes. One cycle can cause or at least affect another; the business developer's responsibility is to know a) that it can happen, b) recognize when it is happening, and c) do something about it.

All of the above having been said, it comes down to the type of buyer (innovator, early adopter, etc.) and do they have the vision, the authority and the budget to make it happen. To the extent that the buyer type is misjudged, the customer creation cycle could be longer.

The Business Developer

The fifth and last determinant of the time and cost of a customer creation cycle is, obviously, the person charged with the responsibility. The technique, behavior and attitude exercised by that person plays directly to the cycle. Elsewhere I've enumerated 21 characteristics of a business developer, each to be rated on a scale of 1 to 10. It's unlikely anyone will earn 10 for all 35, but the higher the overall score, the more probable that their cycle will be as effective and efficient as possible.

Many of those 21 success characteristics can be affected by training, on product, business methodology, technique and attitude. And, just as you don't brush your teeth once and hope it will last a lifetime, you don't train once but rather, often. How often? As long as performance continues to increase as a consequence.

When performance no longer improves with training being part of the equation, it might be time to look at the fifth cycle that is part of this overall picture, namely the life cycle position of the person in question. Business developers have a cycle quite apart from their chronological age. You see it in 15 year olds as well as in 70 year olds. Either one of them can be enthusiastic, eager, energy-driven and looking for opportunity. Or they can be spent, exhausted, and negative, looking at a world of scarcity..

Invariably, a person new to business development — or just new to any opportunity — ill be full of energy, eager to spread the gospel and move forward. Their performance curve, with added training and incentives, looks much like the beginning of any good product life cycle.

And as with that product life cycle, this one also peaks, tapers off, flattens out. Why? Put it down as a mystery of life. Just accept that it happens. Customer creation, after all, is not a passive occupation. Even life-long salespeople seldom sell the same thing all of their sales career. A new product, a new market, a new responsibility. A good business developer thrives on change — and that is a requirement for their careers as well.

If management does not recognize the change in performance for the opportunity it really is, the declining performance business developer will eventually self-destruct —which is truly unfortunate, because it's unnecessary. At the very least, there is a negative impact to the product sales cycle. More importantly, there is an unnecessary negative impact on a human life.

Conclusion

The time from contact to contract and way beyond, as is evident, is determined by much, much more than just what the business developer does when they hit the street. Changing any one or several of the five cited elements can affect the time and cost of creating a customer, proving again that customer creation must be the responsibility of the entire company.

Where to start? That depends on who you are, where you are now, what you want to do or be, and how you want to get it done. Whatever the answers are to those questions, becomes the start-line. You might think it's a good place to be, or not. The reality is that it doesn't make any difference; it's where you are. The question isn't: Is the glass half full or half empty. It's what will you do with the water.

Chapter 8

Communication: Is Anyone Listening

No self-respecting tome on customer creation would be deemed complete without some comment on the subject of communication. It is, after all, the essence of the profession — and yet, we treat it as a given, without regard for its potential and importance.

No gift to mankind is more abused, misused, un- or under-used than the gift of communication. In the world of commerce, the ability to communicate is more important than what you know and maybe even who you know. True communication, when it happens, is mentally invasive. It's getting into someone else's head. It's the ultimate form of intimacy. It's the most powerful tool we humans possess — and undoubtedly the one least understood, developed or perfected.

Contrary to popular belief, the ability to be a good communicator is not some special genius reserved for the likes of Churchill, Lincoln, Hitler and the Dali Lama. We each have all the ability, talent and tools necessary to be great communicators. Yet, at best we converse and at worst it's a monologue. The pity of it is that all the while we believe we are communicating, we're actually engaged in verbal masturbation and don't even know it.

The lack of prior literature

Should one be so bold as to venture into a public library (many of which now serve coffee as a competitive move to Barnes and Noble) and check for books on communication, the category divides neatly into treatises on radio, TV and the Internet on the one hand, and esoteric volumes, complete with quadratic equations to prove their theorems, on the other. The first is the wrong end of this rainbow and the second serves to underscore the assertion that communication is understood about as well as the Loch Ness monster.

Of all the books that even touch on the subject, it's Peter Drucker's MANAGEMENT that provides the best definition. He wrote from the perspective of managers communicating with superiors or subordinates but his analysis applies equally well to any other audience be it customers, investors, suppliers or competitors.

Drucker's thesis

Mr. Drucker makes four observations, all of which ring true. Consult his book for the original text and allow a paraphrase in the meantime.

The first observation is that communication is perception. In other words the communication — if it occurs at all — depends on the recipient, not the sender. The tree falling in the forest absent of people makes no sound, the surf does not exist for the man who is deaf. And if you use terminology — jargon — that your audience does not comprehend, you might as well be speaking Swahili because they don't comprehend that either — and you're not communicating anyway.

It's not a matter of what I said; it's a matter of what you heard. True communication occurs when you have heard what I intended you to hear, when my message sent is the same message you received. Out of the possible fear of exposing their own supposed ignorance, most people will not admit to not understanding a message they fail to comprehend. And another tree falls in an un-peopled forest.

Drucker goes on to say that communication is expectation. We hear what we want to hear, see what we want to see, and when the message received is something we didn't want to hear or see, we either a) ignore it, or, b) twist into something that fits our comfort zone. We all know people who even today say, "I know the Surgeon General said cigarettes are bad for your health; but he didn't mean me," thus displaying all the logic of a dog smelling the fire hydrant before using it for target practice.

So what is one to do with a message that is not expected nor wanted? That's quite common in business development because what you are providing, be it an airplane, a new information system or gene-altered food, is probably better than what it's replacing. All well and good, except what is being replaced is somebody's pride and joy, something that has received time, effort and financial investment. With ego in the balance, the last thing needed is to be told it's no longer needed. There are two schools of thought on how best to handle that message.

The first one advises to let the audience, be it large or small, get prepared for some bad tasting medicine, to sit down, relax, and think before they react. And then you hit them between the eyes with your 2" x

4". In other words, be just as direct and blunt as possible — waste no time or tears. Get it over with.

The second school advises to take a slower, step-by-step approach, what might be called incremental revelation. Pace the release of the facts with the audience's acceptance of those facts. If at any point they begin to reject the presentation, don't go further; just explain and gain their acceptance of where you are. When equilibrium is once again established then move to the next point. Denis Healy, former Chancellor of the Exchequer of the British Government wrote, "When in a hole of your own making, stop digging."

So, when do you use one method rather than the other? The audience and the message sender's relationship to the audience determines that. A partner can send a message that a consultant — much less a vendor — cannot. The sender of the message needs to know the recipient well enough to properly anticipate the re-action. When in doubt, do the incremental — the pace of that can easily be increased, whereas it's difficult to swing a 2 x 4 slowly.

Drucker's third observation was that communication is demanding. True communication is asking the recipient of the message to do something, to believe something, to change and be other than what he/she is. That, Drucker points out, will be successful only to the extent that the message resonates with the listener's values. If it doesn't, it is not believed; it is treated as propaganda. The problem with propaganda is it's contagious — first, one thing is not believed, and then another, and soon nothing from that source is believed. How many people believe a politician? Or a business person? How many people believe the government version of anything? In these days of spin-doctoring, healthy skepticism has reached an unhealthy height.

Drucker's final observation was that communication, while dependent on information, is fundamentally different than information. The latter is best when it is quantifiable, measurable, minimal and unambiguous. Ostensibly, numbers therefore are better than words because there is less chance of misinterpretation. Communication, however, is deemed best when it is multi dimensional, less quantifiable, and the more levels of meaning the better. Indeed, shared experience is the best form of communication. Two people, independently witnessing a sunset, regardless of their ability to articulate, cannot communicate the experience to each other as well as if they had both seen the same sunset and never exchanged a word.

That's why demonstrations of a product are important. That's why trade shows, as ridiculous as some can be, are important. That's why the higher you are on the relationship ladder, the more likely you'll not be replaced by automation — no one has yet been able to share an experience with a machine.

So, communication is perception, expectation, demanding and is related to but different than information. What's difficult about that? It turns out, a lot.

The physiology of speech

Scientists, to the best of their ability in studying the brain, claim there are six steps to producing speech:

- thought planning (what do I want to say?)
- word class organization (does the adjective come before the noun?)
- syntax (arranging the words into a predetermined sequence or so as to be comprehensible)
- syllable selection (in preparation for forming a word)
- word selection (from our internal dictionary)
- intonation, emphasis

And all of this is done without our necessarily doing it consciously. In a split second. Is it any wonder that ever so often we experience a 'slip of the tongue' and say something we didn't mean to say? Or transpose a few syllables?

The flip side of the process are the six steps to hearing:

- start with what was said,
- proceed to what was heard,
- continue through what is recognized,
- and filtered,
- then interpreted,
- and finally understood.

In addition to those two loads of complexity, a further complication stems from a physiological imbalance. For no known reason, humans hear and speak at different rates of speed. The fastest speaking person, in any language, can utter up to approximately 140-150 words per minute — most of us speak much slower, somewhere between 90-110 words per minute. But we can discern the spoken word as fast as 550 words per minute — roughly five times as fast as it normally comes to us.

We know this because tape recorded messages have been increased to two and three times normal speed in an attempt to put more value into the 60 minute distance of the tape. Even with the tone reduced, no one really wanted to concentrate that much. The problem lies in what we do with the extra time between speech speed and hearing speed. With concentrated effort it is possible to focus only on what is being said — but it takes effort. Normally, the listener becomes guilty of mental wandering. The mind has somewhere between 60 and 80 thousand thoughts each day, and they don't necessarily stop just because someone else is speaking. They keep coming unless we consciously channel them to what the speaker is saying. Even then, unless there is a focus on listening, we begin thinking of what to say in response to the speaker. Ego determines that our answer is more important than their presentation, even when the message is interesting and/or important. Worse, if we do not find the incoming message interesting, for whatever reason, we begin wandering and wondering: I wonder what's happening this evening, gee, that was an interesting person I met at the party last night; what are all the things I have to do Saturday around the house; I wonder if I'll make quota this quarter; etc., etc.

The consequence of the speech/hearing speed disparity is that communication becomes anything but a passive sport. It is not something that happens without effort. It takes concentration, focus, intent, willpower, and practice.

It takes more than one to communicate

Apart from fast-talking and/or slow listening, there are several other obstacles to perfect communication, the largest being the imprecision of language. Words are no more than symbols for the realities of our lives. The word "house" is a symbol for what could be a generic house; but when you hear it, the image is probably your house. You've probably not seen my house, nor I yours, so we're immediately talking about two different houses. As I put that commonly understood word, "house" into a sentence, the meaning and definition of "house" will change if I talk about something good that happened in my house, or something unpleasant. In point of fact, house is easily confused with home, an emotion-laden word if there ever was one. Allow me a personal story that might illustrate much of the language challenge.

Back in the mid-60's at the near peak of race related social unrest in the U.S., the financial institution I worked for in the Midwest united with the other leading firms in the city to formulate an initiative to prevent any outward racial conflict in our town. These city fathers, with some wisdom, decided that to the extent the black community could be more gainfully employed, they would be less likely to take to the streets. A plan was devised where every junior manager in all the involved companies would be assigned an unemployed black male and would be charged with getting him a job doing anything, anywhere, for anybody, at any reasonable price.

I took the charge with all the sincerity a naïve do-gooder could possibly muster, intent on re-enacting Daniel in the Lion's Den biblical story. My "client," Jimmy, was a good-looking but somewhat sullen 20 year old high school drop-out who had never held a job, was reasonably sure he'd never be able to get a job because he'd tried and failed, and didn't really relish the neighbors seeing some honkey coming over to visit once a week.

Jimmy lived in a one bedroom house with his mother and 10-year-old kid brother. Two windows had been covered with cardboard to hide broken glass that had yet to be replaced; some of the faucets didn't work for hot water; the back door depended on one hinge which meant opening and closing it was a two-handed operation requiring both strength and quickness. The only good thing about the furniture was that there wasn't much of it. For the most part, I took to standing, leaning against a wall rather than to take a chance on a chair. It was in these surroundings that Jimmy and I spent a couple of hours a week, with me talking about who he was, him talking about what I wasn't, and me again talking about what he ought to be.

With all my smooth-talking, educated white ways, after three months of weekly conversation and my best efforts, I had accomplished absolutely nothing. Quite confident of my own skills, I was ready to write this assignment off as a failure due mostly to the incorrigible character of Jimmy. After all, I reasoned, how can you help someone who doesn't want help? (sounds like a classic sales question, doesn't it?)

Then something happened that I was sure would solve the problem. The federal government announced plans to build a housing project in Jimmy's neighborhood. Large enough for 400 families, with green space for children, bus service for adults, low monthly rent for all and construction to be finished within twelve months. The only inconvenience would be that to clear the area for the new buildings, the present neighborhood was to be demolished, Jimmy's place included. But the feds were going to find temporary housing for everyone while the new buildings were going up.

Here, I thought, was the chance for a new start, an opportunity for all concerned to move up and on with a better way of life. Windows to see through, toilets that flush, doors that swing open and closed. All new, clean and affordable — what more could be asked for?

Jimmy would have nothing to do with it. He said it was a lousy idea and some white probably thinks he's doing us a favor by ripping down the neighborhood. Who do you guys think you are to come and tell us how to live? And what are you really trying to do to us? And on, and on. Nothing I offered as an explanation made any sense to him.

I found myself getting first frustrated, then defensive, and finally angry. I pointed out the advantages of cleaning up the area even if it did mean removing all the residents from what was, in reality, a ghetto. I tried to get him to think about living in a place where the floor didn't sink when you stepped on it, where the wall was one color rather than three, or four, or bare plaster. A real house you could be proud of rather than the filthy shambles he had now. All of which, to me, was evident truth, as plain and simple as the cardboard patch on the missing living room window.

I had just finished one of my "Can't you be reasonable and see what I'm telling you" speeches — ending it approximately 20 decibels above normal conversational tone. And then it was Jimmy's turn. I'd seen him display anger before — but always at the system; now it was directed at me giving a whole new meaning to the word 'seething.' In the next few minutes, in slow but certain terms, he told me why he didn't need no mother f........ honkey destroying his home. That maybe it looks like a ghetto to you smart white guys because you don't live here, with all your money and damn big words, etc., etc. After a long pause, he went on in more quiet tones to explain that on two occasions, when his little brother was much younger and used to sleep on the floor because they had no crib, he, Jimmy, had saved his baby brother's life by sucking the poison out of a rat bite.

Here was a young man who never had a job and the opportunity to prove his performance, who thought he'd never have one because he wasn't good enough, whose only sense of self-value came from what he had done for his little brother — and *that* was possible only because of the house he'd lived in all his life. I called his house a filthy shambles; he called it home. I called the area where he and all his friends lived a ghetto; he called it the neighborhood. I was with the enemy who wanted to destroy the only thing he had for comfort and security, that gave him self-esteem; he had no way of understanding how knocking down houses could be progress.

What was happening here is proof of Drucker's pudding. There had been no perception, we each had totally different expectations, and the demands of each party were equally rejected by the other. The words we both used meant something else for the other. He didn't understand where I was coming from or where I was going, nor did I understand his path. The result? A total lack of communication.

Business — business development in particular — depends on people working together for a common goal. By definition, that requires communication, and words are but a part of that. In fact, as beneficial as a good vocabulary might be, it can be as much a hindrance as a help. It's not just what you say, it's how it's said. Because words are symbols, not reality, they are conditioned by syntax and inflection, prior psychological mindset and stereotyping, source credibility and context.

The words are the same but it's more than syntax that is changed if the question is: "May I pray while I eat?" or, "May I eat while I pray?" A simple phrase like: "They fed her dog biscuits," can have five different meanings just by where the inflection is placed. We each have our hidden belief system which can be triggered by a word or phrase, something that puts us on alert or causes us to drop our guard when our value system is touched. And who will you turn to for nutritional advice, the marathoner with 9% body fat or your overweight high school football coach? Finally, if you need an example of how context affects communication look no further than recent presidential politics where the meaning of "is" was the source of critical debate.

Some general observations

Before concluding that true communication can't take place, allow for it to be possible but within some guidelines and principles.

* First, two monologues do not make a conversation. Nor are two (or more) people having a conversation necessarily communicating.
* Realize that what we hear is interpreted against what we already know. We compare incoming messages with our 'memory bank' of knowledge. The quality of that bank is highly variable, and is made up mostly of second-hand knowledge rather than actual experience. It's something read in the press, or heard from a friend, taught in school, church or the home — but not necessarily experienced first hand. That's neither good or bad. It's just fact.
* Furthermore, we do not look for information until we are ready to use it. If it comes to us before that, we ignore it or misinterpret it. That's not just applicable to yourself; it is also true of your client/prospect/partner. Part of your responsibility if you want to communicate is to prepare the listener for the communication, to manage their expectations.
* And, finally, there is a balance to be achieved between brevity and ambiguity. The briefer the message, the higher the risk of ambiguity. The more definite the message, the longer it's likely to be — but length does not guarantee clarity. The challenge is to achieve communication using as few words as are necessary — no more and no less — and yet to express a complete message, whether that be an idea, concept, feeling, analysis, whatever. This is not a task to be taken lightly.

How to listen

Considering all of the above, it's comforting to know that the best way to determine if you are communicating is to listen to the messages coming back to you in consequence. Ego and reality tell us that we are involved with the message sender; that undoubtedly makes us feel good and it also sets us up to misinterpret the message coming our way. Here are ten rules for improving your listening. They are true for you as well as for the person with whom you are communicating.

1. Disengage yourself. Don't allow yourself to be personally involved. Get out of the transaction and look at it as if you were a third party. This is easier said than done for anyone who's never done it — but it is do-able and provides an interesting, new perspective. If your client is expressing an opinion about your proposal and you're evaluating their comments in terms of how you will spend the commission you'll get, you're not listening. If the client is criticizing some aspect of your proposal and you find yourself taking it personally, you're not listening. Step aside of the situation, as if you were now watching a movie. Try to understand what the client is really saying, and listen to your own response. Is it communication, conversation, or just two monologues?

2. Know that all views — yours as well as others — are partial. The multiple causality that results from interdependency provides the probability for some unknown causes and effects. That, and the possibility of new knowledge, means that nothing is conclusive. Newton was right until Einstein came along. And even Einstein acknowledged his 'truth' would last only until someone else had a better one.

3. Don't expect rationality; accept irrationality. As Elliot Aronson, a noted social scientist, pointed out, "Man is not rational; he is rationalizing. He does not want to be right; he wants to be perceived as being right." Early on in the movie 'The Big Chill,' one of the characters says (allow me to paraphrase): "Do you know what the most important thing in life is? What's more important than good food or sex or anything?" He then goes on the answer his own question with: "I can skip sex for a day, and probably not eat, either - but I can't stop rationalizing. That's impossible — just to stay sane." So, if

we are not rational ourselves, what right do we have to expect others to be?

4. Listen for consequences. Does the message sent cause an effect — and was it intended? Did the message sender want that effect, or was it unintentional? A good communicator intends a consequence, creates a message that causes the consequence. Indeed, the consequence is part of the message and is also the feedback loop that lets the message sender know if the message sent was the message received. Listen, then, to the audience as well as the speaker.

5. And listen to your own response. Was it different than the rest of the audience? If it was, do you know why? And if it was not, do you know why not? What's your relationship to the speaker and did that affect your response? Did you perceive — understand — what was said? Was it what you expected? Did it make any demand of you? How do you feel about all that?

6. Listen for patterns rather than any single point being made. A repetition of an objection, a return to a common theme, similar adjectives and/or verbs (never mind the nouns). A prepared and practiced speech might avoid an evident pattern but normal discourse allows the subconscious to express its patterned self and any pattern, conscious or not, is still part of the substance of the message.

7. Listen for discrepancies, for discord. Some of it is simply irrationality; some of it is very rational but it's still saying something else. A friend once lamented a much needed and desired mountain vacation that she had aborted at the last moment because she couldn't get time off from her job — and then added that she didn't have the money to do it anyhow so it didn't matter. And the kids probably wouldn't have liked it either. Besides, sometimes it's just nice to stay home.

8. And listen for compromise. Listen for the fellow who says: I really want to stop smoking but I can't. Or who says: If I had a choice I'd leave this town. It's probably the same person who said: "I could have gone to college.....:"

9. Know that words, being symbols, have only face value. Listen to the feeling behind the words; note what's happening while the words are being said. As a little kid, when I did something wrong, I knew I'd get a spanking. My dad always started by taking off his belt and saying, "This is going to hurt me more than it will you." He never cried, and I never believed him.

10. And finally, know that listening is only part of receiving a message. All five and even the sixth sense must be involved. Hear, yes, but also watch the behavior; see their body motion — or lack of; what do they do with their eyes, their hands. Do you feel their presence? Does it have enthusiasm? Excitement? Energy? Or is there uncertainty? Doubt? Lack of conviction? All of your senses must be aware. Assume nothing. Hear "cleanly," without the contamination of your own needs or wants or challenges. There is no lack of possible things to do with the empty time between speech/hearing speed. But it might not be the first thing an unfocused mind will turn to. That's why receiving messages takes concentration and effort. To do so, however, is one of the things that will make you a desirable and valuable business partner rather than just a vendor.

Communication is a trained, practiced skill that defies automation, that places you above the noise of the marketplace, that can be the differentiation to set you well apart from the competition. Let the end of selling take place; you've developed the better way to create a customer.

Chapter 9

Setting Objectives

Up to this point, the subject matter has been rules and tools. If the commercial world is changing, new rules and tools are needed. Not all, admittedly, are new; most are just a different way of using what we all knew anyhow (Ecclesiastes 1:19). And in some cases there's certainly a temptation to skip this chapter because the title is 'old hat.'

That might well be the situation right now, because who doesn't know how to set an objective? It's just a matter of knowing what you want to do, isn't it?

That's not a total mistake — just half of one; it's the proverbial one side of a coin. In the commercial world, as important as what you do might be, equally important is what you cause others to do. Nowhere is that truer than in customer creation. Even with all the changes taking place in the market, the basic rules for setting objectives remain the same; however, very few people know how to correctly set an objective. Knowing what you want to do is certainly important but even knowing that leaves you far short of the finish line.

It starts with *writing* the objectives rather than just thinking about them. That results in clarification and increased precision and also minimizes duplication. The most senior and successful business development professionals still do their objectives in *writing* — if for no other reason than the discipline. To not do that is akin to an accountant remembering a balance sheet.

To provide a pattern for your written objectives, follow the simplest little acronym: S - M - A - R - T .

S is for specific
M is for measurable
A is for assignable
R is for realistic or reasonable
T is for time-oriented

Each objective should contain all five elements. If it's not specific, it won't be measurable either, and its more likely to be misunderstood. Because the complex sale involves multiple parties, everyone involved should know who is responsible for the particular objective. The reasonableness of the objective is a judgment call; experience will hone that ability. And an objective without a time frame is more nearly a wish than a plan.

So it's a matter of knowing exactly *what* the objective is, *who* is responsible for it, *when* it should be done, and it ought to be quantifiable and hence measurable because you can then determine *to what extent* it has been accomplished. That's as basic as it gets.

With all that in mind, the most important thing to remember when setting an objective is that it's not what *you* do, it's *what your audience does as a consequence of what you do.*

Let me repeat the point because it's the crux of the entire subject. You can determine your own plan of action, what you want to do and how you want to do it. You can be very aggressive, confrontational, laid back or excited. You can give a 20-minute demonstration, a two-hour presentation, do tricks or stand on your head. And it can all be for naught because you didn't determine what you wanted your audience to do *because* of what you did. That's the missing step in most attempts at setting objectives. If it's not done you have no way to determine if you've been successful, other than judging your own actions, and that's not enough.

For instance, intending to tell a joke, it's possible to do an excellent job of constructing the story, using emphasis and dialect to create the character, build the necessary element of surprise, deliver what you thought was the punch line — and no one laughs. You know you failed because you knew what you wanted your audience to do and they didn't do it. If you didn't know they were supposed to laugh, you might have counted it as a success. Let me hammer away on the point. How do *you* know what to do if you haven't thought through what you want your *audience* to do? In reality, this situation occurs all too often. Have you never made a presentation, answered all the questions, and then asked: "Well, what's the next step?" to which the client answers "I guess we'll think about it, have a few meetings among ourselves and give you a call." You say, "O.K." and leave. Then walking out of their building you turn to your partner and say, "I wonder if we got through to them?"

That you raise the question is probably a good indication that you didn't. If you had set your objectives in terms of what you wanted the client to do you would then know if they did or didn't do what you intended them to do.

That's known as 'terminal behavior,' a term borrowed from the world of education. In school, Dick and Jane must be able to demonstrate a specific amount of knowledge to matriculate from first grade to second. Say, for instance, they must know how to count to one hundred, and have a vocabulary of 25 specific words. If they can do that, they move to second grade; if not, they are recycled.

Likewise, school administrators use the system to also measure the teachers. If one student fails, it might be a student situation, but if half of the class fails it might be a teacher situation. In business development, if the prospect just doesn't seem 'to get it,' it might well be the presenter or the product rather than the audience that is at fault.

A properly worded objective, then, is a positive statement, requiring a consequent action (or reaction) to what you have initiated. The positive statement is required because it is more specific than a negative one; it is enabling rather than constraining. Negatives are not measurable, nor can they be assigned or scheduled.

By requiring an action you more clearly know if you've accomplished the objective because you can witness the result. If the objective were stated as: I want the audience to understand the complexity of their situation, or, I want the audience to think highly of my company, at the end of the day you'll be at a loss to know if indeed they do. How will you know if they understand, or if they think highly? Change the objective to: I want the audience to verbally share with me the three most difficult challenges they face in this situation, or, I want the audience to give me four reasons why they'll do business with my company. Then when you walk away from the meeting, you know if you've accomplished your objective or not.

Now, should it be three of this or four of that? Maybe it ought to be four of this and only two of that; that's not the point of the exercise. It could be two or six or five or ten or whatever. The point is: have a quantified objective that requires action so that you know what you've accomplished. To *have them do* something reflects that they *do* understand the complexity, that they *do* think highly of your company, thus giving you the opportunity to amend, modify, correct, or gratefully approve the result.

So much for the basics. Additionally, the three changes in the marketplace also require a change in the objectives you formulate. When the pace of change exceeds the prospects' learning curve, then an objective involving education of that prospect could well be counter-productive. More detailed information might only further confuse the prospect. Rather than educate, reduce their perceived risk. That might involve education but it could also involve an incremental step-by- step approach to installation, additional support, innovative financing — whatever addresses their sense of risk. And that varies with the individual, risk being personal judgment. I know a high-wire artist who habitually performs before thousands without benefit of a safety-net "because I know what I'm doing" who, at age 38, remains single because marriage is deemed high risk. He doesn't need education, he needs a marriage safety net.

When marketplace competition creates feature/functions in excess of client expectation, then feature/function becomes a given and your objectives shift to consequences, the augmented environments and future expectations and plans, that which differentiates your product/service from whatever the alternative might be. Interestingly enough, very often the discussion will pivot not on product/service knowledge as much as on your knowledge of the client. If all available alternatives are deemed equal, what will cause the decision to go your way? How does that person sitting opposite you think, judge, decide?

And because the Internet and other forms of information dissemination are replacing vendors and sometimes even preferred vendors, you have the continuing opportunity to set objectives in terms of what you want the relationship to be if that would be other than what it currently is. If you've chosen to be a vendor, your objectives are dependent on what you, the salesperson, can bring to the table. As a vendor, your tasks are easier in that you're dealing in features, functions and price. You're not necessarily defining a problem, calculating a return on investment, integrating your solution into a larger environment or affecting your client's corporate goals. You're moving boxes, and your best objectives will be in terms of how you can move more boxes. And to do so before someone realizes there's a less expensive way of doing it without you being involved.

As a vendor, you're carrying a lighter load than if you were a consultant, contributor or partner. You have less to be concerned with but you'll need more prospects (and calls) because you'll lose more sales.

A consultant's best objectives are set in accordance with the questions to be answered. As a consultant, you're viewed as having expertise in a particular area and you are being judged on the basis of responsiveness — how quickly and thoroughly you share your expertise. The objectives, then, involve what you must do to cause them to ask you to do something that allows you to demonstrate responsiveness. If all that sounds convoluted, it's only because it is, but you were the one who chose to be the consultant. Maybe it's time to move up the food chain.

Contributors set objectives in terms of what they want the client to do as a consequence of what the contributor contributes. If your contribution is a suggestion for a new business process, an organizational change, or a new hire, what do you want the client to do with your suggestion? Do you want it implemented? When is it sufficient to merely have it acknowledged (and properly attributed)? Would you ever make a suggestion that you want rejected?

Each of these questions can have a yes or no answer; it's your contribution and you can do whatever you want, which is why it's critical to know what your objectives are. A famous Broadway director once said: "Never go on stage unless you know why you're there. Only then will you be able to let the audience know what you want them to do." Just as an actor communicates with the audience letting them know if they should laugh or cry, so too must you communicate with your client audience, to let them know when to hold or buy..

The best objectives should be shared with the audience that will, knowingly or not, be asked to do something, to respond. Letting them know ahead of time what is expected of them will condition them to a response. Any and probably every audience asks itself why it is an audience. The answer should always be known, never a surprise, and the benefits self-evident. Sharing the objectives, letting them be known, removes any question.

Setting objectives in a partner relationship becomes more complex. Done most beneficially, it is not a unilateral activity. Rather, it is interactive, a shared experience that will say much about the partnership. Each partner exposes his or her vulnerability, his or her soft under-side, and this will be done only with total trust. Each partnership will operate differently because each partner is a different individual and the two or several parts will make for a different whole.

The most productive partnership will be egoless on the part of all parties. That starts with you, because any relationship must start with you. After all, relationships only exist in our mind, and yours is the only one you control. Once the egolessness has been demonstrated and accepted by the several parties, setting objectives becomes a creative discovery/problem solving adventure. What could be more fun? What could be more productive or exciting?

Done properly, setting objectives becomes a fundamental, cornerstone activity in the process of creating a customer. It starts with knowing who I am, a task most of us do not spend enough time on. It's hesitantly or never done because to do so then requires one to act upon the discovery. Invariably, that means change and change is something we usually reserve for the other person to do.

However, knowing who you are allows you to determine how you relate to the client and that in turn aids the determination of the objective. A worthwhile exercise can be to determine how your objectives would change if your relationship changes from vendor all the way up to partner. That demonstrates the consequences of moving up the ladder.

The end of selling has a profound impact on the objectives you set, mostly because you're looking for a different consequence than you formerly had. Your life and your clients' change because you're no longer selling — no longer pushing boxes. Now you're furthering a relationship that eventually will allow you and your client to accomplish something that neither of you could have done by yourselves.

Chapter 10

How to Describe Anything

Here's another one of those conundrums of the business development world: if you have undertaken the responsibility of creating customers for your enterprise, that responsibility will invariably require your describing a number of things: at the very least your product or service, your company and probably yourself. Additionally, you might be required to describe the marketplace, your competitors and any number of other flora and fauna. How does one best do that?

One might think that, given our five senses (six, if we count common), 256 Crayola colors, an average vocabulary of 6,000 words plus or minus a dozen, and then apply whatever number years of life will justify your conclusion, no one would have a problem describing whatever they chose to describe — a house, their job, spouse, products, or the moon. Not so, silver tongue.

Regardless of what is to be described — product, company or self — with rare exception the error made is that our description is a mirror of our mind with little or no attempt to see it from our audience's view point. We usually describe the product as we understand it without regard to the client needs. We describe our company from the point of being an employee — but not from the point of being a customer. And when we do describe ourselves it's at best deprecating or apologetic — and serves no one in the process.

Let's take a structured approach to the task. There are only three variables to the equation: what's being described, the describer, and what for lack of a better word can be called the describee (that's one of the plus or minus 12). That allows for no more than six relationships albeit each with an infinite number of shades of gray. The picture is slightly more complicated by adding Ted Leavitt's (<u>Marketing</u>, The Harvard Press) approach of describing anything at one of four levels:

- generic
- augmented
- expected
- future

The concept Leavitt advanced 30 years ago remains valid, with slight modification necessary to allow for changes in the marketplace.

A *generic* description is the nuts and bolts, bits and bytes, description of the product, service, person or thing in question. It's the summation of physical characteristics, its parts and what it is a part of. If it's a car, the generic description would be: four wheels, two bumpers, six cylinders, one ton of steel, 150 pounds of aluminum, etc. If it's a person, it might be: brown hair, brown eyes (2), 165 lbs., age 29, African-American, etc.

The *augmented* description includes the rest of the package — all the other elements that define this product, service, person or thing. For the product or service it would be how it is delivered, packaged, financed, installed, any necessary training — it might even include a list of references. For a person it would include the amount of education, prior experience, religion, where they live, even salary requirement, or marital status.

The *expected* description is what the buyer/client (describee) really wanted to have or at least to hear. Again, if it's the car, the expectation is usually stated in terms of service, trouble-free operation, trade-in value, etc. If it's a person that is being described, the expectation will depend on the relationship of the three variables (describer, describee, described), all of which will be discussed subsequently.

The *future* description has become as important as the generic or the augmented in today's world of the complex transaction. It must answer the all important question of what's going to happen next Tuesday when I need you? Either the market will change or my needs will change, and I want to know what you're going to do to my benefit when that happens. If it's any product or service, the client wants the assurance of not being left behind. While the need for such a definition seems so evident once mentioned, there is a surprising absence of it in marketing and the marketplace. A complex product or service without an articulable future has as much chance of succeeding in today's commercial world as Boris Yeltsin has of becoming Miss America.

In Leavitt's original work, he visualized the four levels of description as concentric circles with generic being the core, followed by augmented (a bit larger), expected (even larger), and then future. It's debatable as to if augmented is larger or smaller than expected. In much of today's market, augmented product invariably exceeds the clients expectation. How well this is articulated to the prospect is a separate question.

In real life, with a dynamic market, all four circles will change size — and sequence — as the product/service progresses through it's life cycle. If for instance, expectation exceeds even the augmented product, smart management will work assiduously to improve the product, not just to meet expectations but to beat them. Once accomplished, the market's expectations will increase, possibly again exceeding the actual product. And if a company does not meet market expectations, a competitor, as if by magic, will always appear. That's the free-market system we've come to brag about.

From actual experience, it is difficult to imagine a person, product or service, commercial or otherwise, that would not lend itself to Leavitt's descriptive formula. For the professional engaged in customer creation, it's successful use comes as a consequence of its iterative application, *i.e.,* once a good generic description has been put together and used, go back and improve it based on the audience reaction. And then continue to fine tune the description as the product/service/person and the audience change over time.

What's a Product? What's a Service?

To this point in the discussion, product and service have been treated as, if not one, then at least similar. In fact, there is a whole world of difference — but it depends on if you're buying, selling or managing. Again, let's start with the basics.

The essential difference between a product and a service is that a product is defined by its seller and a service is defined by its buyer. Further, the product definition consists of two columns of facts: the first column enumerates what the product is; the second, what it isn't. It then becomes the province of the product manager to determine the validity of what is in the "is" column, and the schedule for moving anything from the "isn't" column into the "is" column.

A service, on the other hand, initially defined by the client/prospect, becomes an agreement between buyer and provider of what the former wants and what the latter can provide.

That is not to say that a service can't be managed, sold and delivered as if it were a product. Likewise, there is an increasing number of products being paraded through the marketplace as services — but the cost of a chosen customization quickly brings one back to buying what is the core product.

Example: if we can avoid an intimate discussion of bodily functions, then possibly the processing of a divorce case would be a good example of a relatively personal service. There is a divorce attorney in Milwaukee, however, who runs what can easily be called a divorce factory. With the aid of a second attorney, two paralegals and a secretary, they process an average of 50 cases a week, month in and month out, with applicants coming from all across the state.

They do it by product management. There is an applicant profile that must be matched; no contested cases, no history of violence from either party, preferably the children are 18 or older or non-existent, etc. Forms are filled out, verified, a comparatively low fee is paid up front. Most cases do not require the parties to attend the hearing. In short, it's cheap and painless. And while the whole thing has been proceduralized, even subjected to cost studies per case, it is presented as a service and delivered as a service.

Conclusion: if divorce can be productized, probably anything can be.

It is management that determines if the transaction is one of product or service. If service is chosen, you can skip the step of developing two lists, *is* and *isn't*. In fact, skip trying to do a generic description because the client provides that in the form of the *expected* definition. If product is chosen, management must then determine if it is to be presented and sold as a service all the while managing it as a product.

In the arena of the complex sale, where the buyer's learning curve and expectations have been exceeded, there is the definite trend to present services as product. The buyer is not defining the offering — it's beyond their knowledge. Defined as a product the offering is more easily understood, it becomes more "visible," real, concrete.

Example: The American business community at this point in time (December, 2000) is preoccupied with gaining a Web presence of one form or another. For those enterprises approaching this challenge for the first time, there is little understanding of what is involved and it becomes the Web developer's responsibility to define the several aspects of the task. Where the client understands having a Web site, they all too often do not realize the intricacies of causing and then building traffic to the site, designing personalization into it, the nuances of navigation, the need for intentional programmed change and the requirement of interfacing their other existing systems to the new Web presence. All of this invariably is tailored to the individual client's situation, needs and requirements, making it very much a service in every sense of that word — except the buyer doesn't know enough to define what needs to be done.

The vendor, therefore, finds it advantageous to describe what's happening in detailed fashion, just as if it were a product that is being delivered. Just as a good surgeon will describe a laparoscopic procedure to the patient before delivering that service. Just as a good gardener will describe what's going to happen to your flowerbed before delivering the first rose.

It would be easy to conclude that, be it product or service, it should always be described as a product, and that might be true but for those situations where the client/prospect really wants to define the deliverable. That will happen whenever the clients know (or thinks they know) as much or more than the product/service provider. But that violates our definition of the complex sale.

Other Factors That Affect a Definition

The type of relationship that exists between client and provider — be that vendor, consultant or partner — should not affect the definition of anything being discussed. Posing as a vendor to a technical person, the generic definition is the same as if you were their consultant or partner. The same would be true for any of the four levels of description or for any of the five levels of relationship.

The description changes only with the audience, and it does so in two separate and independent ways. The first is related to the functional responsibility of the audience; the second is related to the type of buyer (innovator, early adopter, etc.) the audience is.

Example: a computer software system would be described, at any of the four levels, quite differently if the audience is a systems programmer, a CFO, or a president. The programmer is not necessarily interested in ROI or total cost of ownership; the CFO and president are unlikely to comprehend the elegance of structured code any more than a ditch digger is interested in quadratic equations. What is required is a definition geared to the audience and its functional responsibility. Admittedly, this cannot be an iron-clad, formulaic approach. There will always be that programmer who does have an interest in return on investment, just as the occasional ditch-digger knows the value of *pi*. But the general principle deserves consideration.

A possibly more difficult and complex task is to offer any of the four levels of description in terms of the audiences' propensity towards being what Geoffrey Moore *(Crossing the Chasm)* described as innovator, early adopter, early or late majority, and laggard. As was mentioned in Chapter 7, each of these categories of buyers is not clearly evident or apparent. They do not wear labels or live in the same neighborhood. Yet, it can be near fatal to describe a product to an early majority person the same way it is presented to an innovator. As Moore points out in his book, the latter wants a new toy; the former wants a proven product. It's Doom II or a Barbie Doll, and never the twain shall meet.

No wonder, then, that so many people charged with creating a customer do such a poor job in describing themselves, their company and their offering. Done properly, it is not a trivial task. Indeed, it is intellectually and creatively challenging — plus being a task that is, while critical, never finished.

How to Describe Yourself

A truism in the commercial market is that the procedure for creating a customer does not start with the product/service being offered or even the company that produces the offering; it starts with the person engaged in the business development activity. That person who represents the company and product must first be accepted as credible or no transaction will take place. Whether this is accomplished verbally in the first person, by performance over time, through third-party testimonials or, more likely, by all three, it starts with the individual knowing him or herself — and then being able to articulate and demonstrate that person to their several daily audiences. (Intelligent third-party name dropping is allowed if done with purposeful panache.)

While it takes on the appearance of being a manipulative actor to say that one must accommodate several different audiences, the truth of the matter is that one deals with the six-year-old son differently than a client/partner or a competitor. But it's not the core person that changes; it's merely the delivery of a message geared to the current audience. The ability to do that is quite apart from knowing your core values and knowing yourself.

It's fair to conclude that the majority of the world's people, at any given moment in time, are clueless as to who they are. Look around in a shopping mall, or an airport, or anyplace where there are many people. How many faces have an expression of purpose, goal, action or accomplishment? The occasional one or two look as out of place as prime rib in a vegetarian restaurant.

From another angle: define charisma — not the dictionary definition, but what is it that causes that singular person to be charismatic? What causes the room atmosphere to change when that person comes through the doorway? It's how they carry themselves. It's that they make eye contact with each person they look at — it's not a casual glance — they speak with their eyes. Most often they do not speak loudly — they don't need to. They move through the room, or let the room move through them, but either way, it is with purpose. There's no physical characteristic that defines the charismatic person and if there were one word needed to describe him or her, it would be: intense.

Not tense; not uptight — anything but. They're not necessarily moving fast or talking loud — if they are, it's for a purpose. Indeed, it's possible to say that they lead their life 'on purpose.' And that radiates to and through their audience irrespective of who the audience is.

Charisma does not come from title or position, nor is it inherited or assigned. Its possession is sometimes self assumed when in fact it is non-existent. It is independent of vocation, age or gender, as well as race, creed or national origin. And it's not *what* you believe; it's *that* you believe — in yourself, in what you're doing, in where you're going. That means it has only one source: the individual who has it. And, by definition, that can be anyone. Whoever that is, it will be a person who knows him or herself.

So what does one have to know about themselves? Daniel Goleman has written several books on that one subject and according to him the basics of personal competency are:

- self-awareness — knowing one's internal states
- self-regulation — managing ones internal states, and
- motivation — the emotional tendencies that aid one in realizing goals

All three rest on a value system that guides the person in setting priorities and determining what actions to take. The challenge in all of this is that much of our action is spontaneous and/or unconscious — that is, we seldom think through what's to be done before we do it. As another social scientist, Elliott Aronson, said a long time ago: we do or we don't and then we make up reasons why we did or didn't.

Further, in acquiring any earned skill, we pass through four stages that can be represented as follows:

	Incompetence	Competence
Unconscious	1	4
Conscious	2	3

We start by being unconscious of our incompetence. That is, we don't know what we don't know. We then progress to a conscious incompetence — we become aware of what we don't know. And then move, hopefully, to a state of conscious competence. Here, we can exercise the skill or knowledge but it requires concentrated effort to do so. Finally we arrive at the point where we can exercise our competency without the concentrated effort.

Think of your learned experience in driving a car — and realize that the majority of accidents today take place because the people were in stage four, they weren't aware of what they knew too well how to do. Piano players fall into stage four; pianists are in stage three. Recreational tennis players are fours; Sampras and Hingis are threes.

The point of the exercise is: are you consciously aware of your competencies or are they under the control of your autonomic nervous system; that is, do they just happen? Further, do you know your value system to the point of being able to articulate it? Can you easily set priorities, determine what's important versus what's urgent? The ease of these tasks is determined by the clarity of the underlying values and your ability to practice them.

And fundamental to all of it is your 'walking the walk as well as talking the talk.' When you blithely declare that family is more important than career, name the last three situations where family came before staying the extra two hours at the office or when business did not determine when you took your vacation or days off. As the self-proclaimed risk-taker, give three examples of the risks you have taken. As the self-proclaimed decision maker, give three examples; and then give three more where the decision was a bad call. And for those who claim being responsible for their own lives, explain what caused those three decisions to go bad.

Being able to define and describe yourself is not an easy nor trivial challenge. To step outside of your daily situations and examine yourself as a third party is nonetheless a very worthwhile exercise.

Start by writing a list of what you have done for yourself. Do a second list of what you've done for others. Each time, attempt to be exhaustive. Then list what you have. When that list is finished, go back and classify the items as tangible or intangible, and draw a conclusion as a consequence. Finally, put into writing what you want to be, what you want to do with your life, and what you're doing to make it happen.

With all that as prologue, describe yourself using Leavitt's four levels — generic, augmented, expected and future. It's quite possible that little of the resulting description will change to accommodate a different audience. A good self-description should be universal.

The importance of this exercise cannot be over-emphasized: It is the first and primary building block of any relationship; it will always be a work in progress; it defies being automated.

As for the school that says: you only have one chance to make a first impression, the response is: so what? Relationships are built on experiences and trust, tempered by time and discovery. First impressions are but one step of a multiple-step process.

How to Describe Your Company

Now the commercial plot thickens. All four levels of description for the company can be cobbled together by the senior copy writer in the marketing department, posted on the company Web site, and summarized in the leave-behind brochure that is invariably handed out too early in the initial meeting. Admittedly, most of those word mongers do a fairly adequate job on the generic level, put a modicum of effort with consequent result into the augmented level, use whatever market research has produced for the expected description, and push the envelope of adjectival reasonableness when describing tomorrow.

What can-not be canned by those English majors is the relationship to the company of the business development person who is sitting in the client's office. Just as a person reveals something about his marriage by the way he describes his spouse (and vise-versa) so too does he reveal something about his company by describing his relationship with that company, something that can't or won't ever be put into a brochure or on the Web.

More than the promotional jargon and hype consequential to an over-used Roget's Thesaurus, the client wants to know what your company can and will do because of you and your relationship with it. Any expressed negatives, however true they may be, become a red flag. Likewise any positives will require authentication by example. Your enthusiasm or hesitancy is interpreted in terms of your ability to influence your company on behalf of your client. Whether or not you are a happy camper with regard to your employer has impact only as it is perceived to affect the client's interests.

Start by becoming intimately familiar with whatever the marketing department has generated to date, on all four levels. Fill in the blanks for anything you feel is missing, and relate yourself to those descriptions with examples that illustrate the several points. Then take it the next step by describing your corporate personality and culture. Is the company energetic, youthful, passionate about its chosen mission and product offering? Is it leading edge, tried and true, conservative, flexible, responsive, aggressive, stable, etc. etc. With each adjective, provide the commensurate example that proves the point.

If in this process, it is not possible to wax enthusiastically and appreciatively about the organization you represent, attempting a cover-up will only jeopardize your own credibility. Better you should a) be truthful and attempt to influence or cause a change within the company, or b) polish your resume and prepare for a new opportunity. Clients can sense vagueness for what it is the way animals can sense fear.

Any description of the company must relate to the client audience. Operations staff are interested in other things than what the CFO or president are. Furthermore, innovators need a different description than an early majority buyer. How the description changes is dependent on what product or service is being discussed, but that it changes is a given.

In the end, the client wants to know, believe and understand that the company and its representative, whether the title is sales person, business development manager or trail boss — have a solid, mutually productive and enjoyable relationship. Pride in the organization and its leadership, enthusiasm for its mission and satisfaction with its accomplishments are much more important than longevity or even size.

The professional business development person intent on creating customers will put a significant amount of effort into describing these three basic components of the complex sale, their product/service, themselves, their company. It is not an incidental task, nor can it just be part of the marketing literature. It's the stuff that relationships are made of.

The same attention must be paid to any description that is required in the process of creating a customer. It is an admittedly intellectual challenge. It is also creative, exciting and rewarding. And something that can't be automated.

Chapter 11

Name Three Compelling Reasons To Buy

Depending on the approach you want to take, there are probably many more than three reasons. If there are four levels of description for what you're selling (generic, augmented, expected, future) and five types of buyer (innovators, early adopters, early majority, late majority and laggards), then there are at least 20 reasons needed to satisfy that matrix. Given that a reason to buy could be stated as a feature/function, a benefit or a consequence, you should have 60 reasons.

It's doubtful if you'll ever need 60 reasons, compelling or otherwise but it might be worth the exercise to draw the matrix and see how many squares could be filled. Even allowing for some redundancy, it could be a challenge. Odds are, the matrix could be completed for any given product or service — but not all reasons would be compelling (defined by Webster as irresistibly interesting, attractive, captivating). Some of those 60 reasons will border on the mundane and ordinary, anything but interesting and as captivating as yesterday's oatmeal.

The key is in knowing more than just the definitions of the four by five by three terms in the three dimensional matrix. In addition to that analytical approach look at it from a systems point of view.

If every system gets its value and purpose from the system it is a part of, then what is the larger system(s) your product is part of? And how does your product (system) impact that larger or other system? To put a value on the impact, you need to first know what situation you're resolving. Was the prior system broken, not working, causing damage and pain or is your fix a nice-but-not-necessary?

A non-functioning system can cause pain of varying degrees to various members of the group. Who feels what pain? Do you know any of the multiple causes (there's always more than one) of the pain?

Any problem has three costs: the cost of *having* the problem; the cost of *solving* the problem — that is, implementing the solution; the cost of *not solving* the problem. How well do you understand all three of those, and does your client understand them as well? Often it is the salesperson's thankless and somewhat difficult task to enumerate these cost equations because the prospect is too close to the situation and hasn't taken the time or energy to step back an honest distance to evaluate the situation.

Lastly, it helps to know who benefits from a solution, and how they benefit. Seldom will a solution provide equal benefits to all. Multiple benefits, yes; equal, seldom if ever. Indeed, there will be times when a member of the group gets no benefit other than seeing his cohorts satisfied. Few people are pleased with being in that position unless a childhood of losing at musical chairs and playing wall flower at the Senior Prom has adequately prepared them for it.

A business development person invariably has the opportunity to assess the situation and know who benefits and how, and who might not be benefiting as much as they feel they deserve. Recognizing the short-changed, real or imagined, you can then address that situation rather than let it go unanswered. As has been said: Never underestimate the power of the abused minority.

Now go back to the 4 x 5 x 3 matrix and with all the perspective gained from the questions just asked, put a reason in each of the 60 boxes. Any reason, realizing that as you move through the matrix you'll come back and change/upgrade some of your answers.

So, what's the generic, feature/function reason an innovator would have to buy your product? Or an early adopter? etc. Then see if you can name a benefit, and then a consequence to that innovator, etc. And if the honest answer is "NONE," accept it.

Don't attempt to do it in any particular sequence. Jump around — answer what seems obvious to you or what you've had experience with. Be redundant if it is called for and see if that gives you a pattern of any kind. Patterns can tell you something about your product and its audience that in turn will allow you to be more effective and efficient.

Just a note: Hardly anyone will quibble about the need for effectiveness; that's one of those qualities we all like to think we have in abundance but we're still prepared to have more of. Efficiency however, causes some people distress. Maybe it sounds as if we're designing a non-human system, that we're ratcheting up productivity in a machine.

In part, that's true, but only because efficiency has to do with time, and time is the great constraint we all face. Much of our individual — or joint — success is dependent on what we do with each 24 hours given us in a day. You might not have enough hours in the day to be a successful salesperson, mother, homemaker and neighbor. Another person has enough time in those same 24 hours to run Hewlett-Packard. How you choose to use your 24 hours does make a difference. In that context, efficiency becomes very important.

At the point in your matrix development that you feel you've reached the nadir (or is it the apogee?) of diminishing return, switch to identifying the *compelling* reasons. Which ones are really important? Which ones are multi-dimensional, basic, pivotal, affect more than one other system, have the greatest ROI, the least cost, the shortest implementation schedule, etc., etc.? Use as many metrics as you choose — providing they are all valid.

It's more important that you have a compelling reason for each of the five prospect types than for each of the four product definition types. And the higher you are on the 'relationship ladder' with your prospect, the more likely the compelling reason will involve a consequence rather than a feature/function.

As with several other items, *Compelling Reasons to Buy* are the consequence of thoughtful study and experience on the part of the business developer. And as that credit card ad points out, never leave home without them.

Your *Compelling Reasons to Buy* should be an automatic response, something you can easily verbalize, without hesitation, whenever the situation calls for it. Keep the explanation and justification of each compelling reason as paragraph two; the reasons should be brief and to the point, easily remembered and repeatable.

And be prepared to adopt a new or additional compelling ceason any time a prospect/client offers one. Not all will be worth keeping; some will be usable only with the client who offered it (if it's important to that prospect, it's important to you); and occasionally you'll get the well-turned phrase that you can use over and over again. The prospect/client that does that for you should get special treatment at the next Annual Users Conference.

With rare exception, most sales people short-change the significance of the economics of the transaction they are driving. One would like to think business development people could and would better understand the importance of those economics but that's a misguided assumption. We've been so conditioned to "look for who has the pain" that we don't realize that a healthy company might not have pain - but it always has its economics. Even if the buying decision is made at a technical level, rest assured that it will be screened and evaluated by someone with an economic eye.

First off, recognize that economics is a multifaceted jewel; one person's return on investment will be another's market share and yet another's product cycle time. The initial task then, is to focus on what the client cares about. How to find out? Ask. The first categorization is whether the person is concerned with cost reduction or revenue improvement. Some might ask for both. You need to be clear on what your product/service can deliver. And if you can express it in quantified terms.

If another client was able to reduce inventory by 25% and increase inventory turn from six to eight times a year, what was the dollar impact? If sales increased by x number of dollars, what did that mean to market share? Note that we're talking consequences, not just benefits. And we're talking what for some will be very proprietary, confidential numbers — so much so that the client will be hesitant to disclose the actual in other than vague terms. The business development person can nonetheless spell out the equation to be used and speak in relative terms: "If you can reduce inventory by 2%..."

Knowing your client's industry leads to knowing their economics - their cost points and their revenue sources. The possible metrics are many: ROI, return on equity, inventory turns, market share, product cycle time, cost avoidance, cost reduction, revenue increase, etc. The list goes on and on and can become highly individualistic. Burger King used to measure new costs in terms of how many more hamburgers they'd have to sell; a door and window sash manufacturer in Milwaukee knew his daily profitability based on the number of barrels of scrap lumber he had at five p.m.

Your success rests on knowing your audience's metric — whatever is important to them - and then being able to quantify it, hopefully in terms of their own finances. To do that requires being more than a vendor, and probably more a consultant. The ultimate goal is to be able to impact the client's bottom line, the P of their P & L. Maybe your product/service doesn't carry that kind of impact; maybe your client is so large that your impact in only visible at a departmental level rather than corporate. Whatever your metrics, know them.

The exercise of determining where it fits, or if it fits, will carry its own reward even if it doesn't fit. You'll learn more about the product/service that you're offering, and more about the client. And the client will learn more about you. In the process, you're approaching partnership status, and minimizing the possibility of being replaced by a clever on-line information system.

Chapter 12

Putting It All Together

My Grandmother had a recipe for chocolate cake that began with "steal two eggs".... It did not specify whether the victim was a neighbor or a chicken. Grandmother explained that it just demonstrated the importance of using two eggs regardless of how difficult it was to get them. And that's how a recipe for anything should start — with the most basic and important thing first. For Grandma's cake that meant two eggs; if you didn't have them, it wasn't going to be a cake.

So it is with anything new — even a new recipe for creating customers. We've been creating them for a few thousand years, but now there are some new ingredients, it's a new kind of oven, even the clock is different and, most importantly, the audience has changed. Yet most people are still using the same old recipe, wondering why it doesn't turn out the way it had in the past.

Well, what's to be done? What is the basic and most important thing? It's time to test your risk threshold. Yes, change requires risk and it comes at a price. So does not changing, particularly when the world around you is and you're not. I found out a long time ago that whenever I took a formal tennis lesson — to improve my serve, or ground stroke or whatever — it screwed up my game for the next several times I played. But if I stayed with it I ended up with a better game. To the extent you change any aspect of what you're doing now to create a customer, there will probably be some set backs before you get it right. But that's OK; know that you'll be ahead in the end.

Would that there were no existing constraints, no current barriers or baggage to overcome or remove. Unless you're in a start-up company, there is not the luxury of a *tabula rasa*. That doesn't mean change can't take place; it just means it takes place on two levels: at the individual, personal level; and at the corporate level. Which comes first? It doesn't matter. What matters is that *something* comes first.

Step One

To begin with, no one should interpret the end of selling as a justification for laying back, taking it easy, sit and watch the Fords go by. It's anything but — indeed, to the extent the switch is made, that business development person will find himself more involved, more active, probably busier than ever before, because success has its own intensity, its own energy, its own high. Rare is the person who wants to quit when she's winning; invariably, it's the other way around. It's after the 10th NO for the day. It's knowing that 200 calls are needed to make one sale and the only way to get a second sale is to make 400 calls. That doesn't sound like a winning formula.

The oft-repeated story about Edison trying more than 1000 different materials to get a filament for his light bulb is a bit skewed. The reality is he had 50 engineers working in his laboratory and *they* tried the 1000 times — and I'm willing to bet my socks not one of them ever said: "Oh, goodie. That didn't work." Show me a person who enjoys losing and I'll show you a loser. Or a Chicago Cubs fan.

Changing your approach to your market is not to be done without careful consideration. It's been said that people will change only if the consequences change. The example usually given is one of a person, late for work, driving on the Interstate, exceeding the speed limit by a bit more than the 12 mile-per-hour margin tolerated by la guardia civil. A squad car appears in this driver's rear view mirror and he immediately seeks to become invisible. He slows down, moves into the right lane, preferably between two trucks and refuses to look in his rear-view mirror until he sees the squad car go past him.

Several miles down the road, he gets a flat tire. He pulls over to the shoulder and, not having a cell phone is faced with flagging down another vehicle, most of which are also exceeding that 12 mile-per-hour margin. Then, as if in answer to a prayer, another squad car appears in his field of vision and, suddenly, this person who attempted deprivational dwarfism six minutes ago is welcoming the police like a long lost brother. Even close inspection would lead you to believe it was a different person.

And so it was. The behavior changed because the consequences changed. It works every time. Sales managers know this when they develop commission plans. And that's what anyone is doing when they are creating a customer; the client is changing their behavior because they see a better consequence for their having done so.

Rather than steal two eggs, the first task in moving to a new approach of customer creation is to understand, know, believe the consequences of doing that. Sound simple? It is; but this time simple is not easy. Change seldom is. The key to accommodating change is to make it a constant, an always present process rather than an occasional event. I stopped losing a half dozen games after a tennis lesson when I began going to a tennis clinic twice a week. Change became an always activity.

We've all heard it throughout our careers: "The only constant is change itself." Hearing it is one thing; making it part of your existence is another. Saying: "What, another change?" is replaced with "Wow, something new." Rather than facing change, embrace change; don't confront it, welcome it; see it as an opportunity, not an obstacle. For some if not most, this will be a paradigm shift in attitude, but the consequences are so overwhelmingly beneficial as to preclude hesitation.

Think what it would mean to really enjoy every day, to know that you have eliminated uncertainty in your activity, that clients *want* to see you and have you involved in their work. Do you get a 'high' from success? Do you know you can have that feeling every day, not just once in a blue moon?

It's all up to the individual. We speak of the gate-keepers in our careers and professional life, usually referring to them as the people who keep us from success, who block our path, who deny us our destiny. In fact, the biggest gate-keeper is invariably, ourselves.

Step two

Once you've convinced yourself that you are capable of success, turn to your client base — both prospective and actual — and rank them as to the relationship you have, with the individuals you deal with within the enterprise, and then with the overall enterprise in general. For every answer you give, cite an example that proves the choice, be it vendor, partner, consultant, etc.

This is not a trivial exercise; it's building the foundation of your move into a new way to create customers. After you've identified and ranked each relationship, look for patterns. Are the majority of your relationships that of *vendor*? Are any *partners* only with lower level staff? Are you stuck in a *consultant* role, not knowing how to move up the food chain to *contributor*?

Having found the pattern, or the lack of one, formulate a strategy to move each of those relationships up one level. Determine the exact action(s) you will take to cause that relationship to improve, and note what action(s) the client will take that let's you know that there is improvement.

You'll want to keep a client-by-client record of all this. Time stamp every entry you make. Reveiew the records no less than monthly. Treat it as you would your financial records, because, in a sense, that's what it is — your path to greater success.

So far, it probably sounds like a lot of work. So far, it is.

Step three

There's one more mental exercise that will help the process of changing to this new method of creating customers. It involves the cycle required to perform this act of commercial magic.

As expressed in previous pages, every product or service will have a minimum number of steps to be executed to transform a prospective user into a client. There can be more than the minimum; some business developers will have more steps than others due to their personality or particular approach; and some cycles will have unnecessary redundancy either purposely built in or negligently allowed. The objective of formulating the cycle is to minimize the elapsed time in balance with least cost and maximum return. (And you thought playing MONOPOLY was fun!)

The challenge now is to take whatever steps are in the cycle you are now practicing and toy with how they might change, what you could or would do differently if you enjoyed a higher level of relationship with your client, person or company. The prime objective relates to elapsed time and costs, but just as important might be the pleasure, enjoyment and/or satisfaction you and the client derive from the process. After all, no one ever said work had to be synonymous with drudgery.

All three steps are rather simple and basic: 1) who am I? 2) what's my relationship with my client? 3) what's different if I change that relationship? On the one hand it has some of the characteristics of a children's parlor game, say, musical chairs: 1) Where *was* my chair? 2) What's everyone else doing? 3) Now where am I?

The big difference is the consequences of the client relationship game are more important, by a factor of twice the square of your zip code. We're talking career-altering activity here, major financial improvement, and significant personal change, behavioral modification way past brushing your teeth *and* your shoes everyday.

The other side of the coin

All of the above can be more easily done if you are the only person in the company charged with the responsibility of customer creation, or if you have a start-up company and you're building new infrastructure. Odds are, however, that if you're not the manager, you'll need a manager who recognizes the new customer creation equation — and changes management practices accordingly. What must change? Let's start with the hiring process.

Defining the job

If someone said there were five different types of jobs that could be called selling — and that we are referring to as business development or customer creation — someone else would say there are at least ten. And if it started with ten, someone else would say twenty. There probably is no known number of ways to slice that cucumber but one thing is for certain: it's more than one. Yet, when it comes to describing the sales job for purposes of attracting a candidate we all too often speak in generic terms, as if sales is sales.

Not so, word-monger; everything you've read up to this point should help to identify the different business development environments that exist. To help sort it out, answer these kinds of questions:

- Is the buying process impulse, simple or complex?
- Is the product new or well established in its marketplace?
- Is the audience business or consumer? Local, regional or national? Hi-tech or low?
- How well defined is the target audience?
- How large is the target audience?
- What is the practiced cycle of activity for creating a new customer? Or, is there a practiced cycle?

- How is that cycle initiated? Who is involved?
- What's the product's price point?

All the answers help to define the job of creating a customer for a particular product or service, but that's just the beginning of the definition.

Add to the above a list of the responsibilities that go with the job: Travel? prospecting? Size of territory? Support provided? Marketing materials?

And just as importantly, what are the objectives and expectations of management? Initially? Over the first year? For the forseeable future? And if expectations are missed, met or exceeded, what's the reward or consequence?

Finally, any good candidate will want to know the future of the job. What are the advancement possibilities? Is there a career with this opportunity or is it just a good way to make a lot of money?

There are no right or wrong answers to any of these questions. It's merely a way of describing the opportunity so that it can be matched to the proper applicant. Know, and believe, that for every job opportunity there is a matching applicant (just as there is a man for every woman, proof of which is evident anytime you observe couples in a shopping mall, or any crowded street.) The challenge is to describe the job in enough detail so that an adequate match is possible.

Define the candidate

Not only is there a tight labor market out there, the market for skilled, proven business developers is near impossible. Consequently, it seems most employers are ready to settle for any warm body with a modicum of related experience and an IQ that approximates room temperature. Ferreting out the experience and education is done rather well, because it's factual and can be verified. It's also the least of the three factors involved in finding the right job candidate. The other two are: talent and chemistry, or more completely: talent and traits, and chemistry and characteristics.

Many managers have difficulty interviewing to determine these factors. Asking direct questions will elicit no more than the obvious answer. Are you honest? Intelligent? Hard working? What person looking for a job would have anything but an affirmative response? If they told you the truth you might not hire them. Besides, do you know anyone who feels they are anything other than above average?

Forget the direct question approach; go for the examples. It's story-telling time. Give me an example of the most difficult sales situation you've ever had. Have you ever had a client who wanted you to do something underhanded, even illegal? What did you do about it? Some clients' pride themselves on 'cutting a deal', getting a discount. In your experience, what's the best way to handle that?

It starts by having a relatively clear idea of the kind of person you want representing the company, indeed, representing you. How aggressive a person do you want? What kind of image do you want to present to the marketplace? What are you trying to accomplish and what are you willing to do to get it done? What does your audience expect, and want? And does it make a difference?

Having various people in your company participate in the interviewing process can also answer the question of if the candidate will fit into the corporate culture, if they have the right chemistry. Every company has one, whether by design or happenstance. Even if you haven't put it into written form, your corporate culture is daily practiced by your employees — and management.

If you want to continue the culture you have, current employees will provide a valuable litmus test for the candidate. Whether they interview casually or by structured questionnaire, the employees will either accept, reject or put the candidate on hold (which in cultural terms is equivalent to rejection).

If you want to change the culture, current employees will probably not play much of a role. First, find out whose side they're on; a vote for the status quo invalidates their interviewing role. It could go farther; cultural change frequently requires housecleaning and restructuring, but that's a dicey game and not to be played by the feint of heart.

Very often, the sales and marketing department of a company will, by dint of leadership and organization, have a different culture than the rest of the company. IBM for instance, for a large part of its existence, was lead by a management made up of people who rose through the field sales organization. It thus became, for better or worse, a self-perpetuating system and worked well — to a point. Incest in any form has its known consequences.

Of the three criteria (talent, experience and chemistry) the ideal candidate will have a balance of all, with no one being dominant or providing the deciding factor. If something must be sacrificed, let it be the experience and education. As the new employer you can provide those whereas talent and chemistry tend to be binary in nature; they are either there or they aren't and whatever they are probably won't/can't be changed by anything short of a frontal lobotomy.

If the candidate has only one of the three, regardless of which one it is, don't hire him. Particularly is this true if you are to choose experience with an absence of talent and chemistry. That's an accident on its way to happening.

The talent and behavior traits necessary to get the job done; the chemistry — personality — that matches the company culture; and then the experience and education that will provide the edge of greater productivity. Hiring and then retaining the *right* employees, not just the brightest, is the basis of any successful business development effort. The more effort put into hiring, the less effort is required for retaining. Never hesitate to use outside testing and interviewing; as expensive as it might seem, it won't hold a candle to the cost of hiring the wrong person. (Every major city has at least one behavioral testing resource, some better than others, any better than none.)

Make training part of the job

The all too familiar process of putting a new sales person in place is to attempt to hire only experienced people, give them a product/service brochure to read and then turn them loose, invariably with quota expected to be met the first month. That's about as realistic as expecting a shut-out to be pitched by a six-year-old because he's wearing a baseball cap.

Training comes in at least four sizes or colors. First, there's the obvious need to explain the product/service being offered, undoubtedly in its four levels (generic, augmented, expected, future), probably with a bit of history as to where it came from and why.

Secondly is the matter of marketplace. This is not just the territory to be covered — as important as that obviously is — it's also the characteristics of the market: how big, how many, their demographics, the level of sophistication, how decisions are made, etc. It's also the

105

competitive landscape and the competitive advantages you have, or don't have.

Then comes an explanation of the sales cycle. Quite often, there isn't one, or if there is, it's unreasonably simplistic, more the consequence of wishful thinking than documented experience. Whatever it is, it should be presented and discussed and the new hire should be encouraged to develop a cycle that fits their personality and style.

If the training has gone this far, it's appropriate to explain company process and procedure. How is an order processed? Who approves the order? How is it fulfilled? Who is involved if something goes wrong? What about reporting procedures and sales meetings and technical support and management involvement, etc. And don't forget to explain when and how commissions are paid, expenses re-imbursed, and travel arrangements made.

Somewhere in the plan there must also be an allowance for on-going training, on all of the above and for new techniques and methodology, as well. Any and all of the elements of a business development person are subject to continuous and unpredictable change. As management becomes aware of these, that information must be shared with those charged with customer creation.

Metrics

Grandpa used to say: If it ain't measured, it won't happen. And, as usual, he was right. Whether it's a clock or a yardstick or a cash register, performance and accountability go hand in glove. Anyone who avoids being measured should not be given the job.

That said, do we know how and what to measure in this new realm of customer creation? Step one is to separate activity from performance and, if you must, judge each separately. Then make a management decision on rewarding on gross revenue or on profitability. Taking no-margin orders won't produce a profit but might keep the plant busy; therefore, doing so is sometimes a prudent move — as long as it's done consciously. And a thin margin order to satisfy a competitive bid situation from a long-standing client can be acceptable when put in the context of the lifetime value of the client, done consciously.

Please note that we're talking about different metrics than the usual gross revenue numbers that are standard fare. A partnership client is likely to have a higher lifetime value than a client that has only a vendor relationship. That undoubtedly should be measured, and rewarded. The person who can reduce the elapsed time in a sales cycle should be measured, and rewarded. All other things being equal, a higher profit margin sale should have a larger reward.

Now, the old guard will say we're making it too complicated, that commission plans have to be simple so that a.) the salesperson can understand them and b.) the company can administer them. While there is an element of truth in both statements the real need is for intelligence rather than simplicity, and if we can put three men on the moon, it seems reasonable to expect that we can administer any commission plan.

All of the above, from hiring practices through commission plan planning is what is setting business development management farther apart than ever from the actual field work it manages. To go from field to manager is anything but a one-step move. It needs to be a transition that involves further training and a new perspective.

What else?

For all the hype and some of the nonsense that has circulated about 'the new economy' and the so-called business revolution, recognize that the impact of the Web with its Internet Protocol can be summarized into two words: access and process. It is a communication system, no more and no less, that allows greater and quicker access and process of information.

Use it for what it is. Communicate more immediately with your field force, clients and prospects. Put as much of your feature/function information as possible on the Web, secured or unsecured, as your comfort level allows. Demonstrate your product on the Web; take orders on the Web use it as another distribution channel to whatever extent possible. Incorporate the Web into your overall marketing and sales strategy — and know that as a consequence you will need to change many of your existing strategies. And tactics. And expectations. And procedures. There's a whole new book that can be written about that.

Your basic approach to business remains the same — except you can get things done easier and more quickly. It should be easier to establish a higher position on the relationship ladder; you can get answers back to your client more quickly, often better response to time-sensitive challenges, reduce cycle time for product development and delivery, and all of this for the same or lower cost.

But the pace of change, process and progress in no way invalidates the basic business equations. Brand equity is still built on a promise kept, not on the number of eyeballs coming to your Web-site. The sustainability of the business still depends on revenue exceeding expense rather than the questionable patentability of century old business processes.

Integrating your customer creation activity with Web capability is a wise competitive move. It's not rocket science. It need not be mysterious or frightening. The changes it will force will result in a better business process.

And is it the end of selling?

Yes, as it has been known, and not a moment too soon. We've lived in the old paradigm of sales long enough to have corrupted its image and violated its importance. If changing the rules, tools and process as well as its related semantics results in a new cake and a new frosting, then Grandma was right. Start by stealing two eggs.

APPENDIX

- 21 Characteristics of a salesperson

- Mandela inaugural quote

- Mountain Dreamer statement

Self Evaluation Chart

As dispassionately as is possible, rank yourself on the following 21 points. Use one as the lowest and Ten as perfect; and when you're finished, see how close or far your score is from 210. There's no winning or losing to the exercise; it's just a way for you to set a benchmark so that six months later you can do the exercise again — without first referencing the one you did 6 months previously — to determine what's changed.

Product knowledge
Company knowledge
Market knowledge
Understanding the sales cycle
Territory management
Lead generation
Using the telephone
Information gathering
Letter writing
Handling objections
Closing
Post sale activity
Time management
Presentations/Demonstrations
Proposals
Setting objectives (for the call)
Organization
Prospecting
Record keeping
Strategizing
Business acumen

:

The following is a quote used by Nelson Mandela in his 1994 inaugural address as President of South Africa. He's not talking hubris; he's talking about truly knowing who you are.

Our deepest fear is not that we are inadequate...
Our deepest fear is that we are powerful beyond measure.
It is our light, not our darkness that most frightens us.

We ask ourselves, who am I to be brilliant, gorgeous, talented and fabulous.
Actually, who are you not to be?

You are a child of God.
Your playing small doesn't serve the world.
There is nothing enlightened about shrinking so that others won't feel insecure around you.
We are born to make manifest the glory of God within us.
It's not just in some of us; it's in everyone.

And, as we let our light shine, we consciously give others permission to do the same.
As we are liberated from our fear, our presence automatically liberates others.

I don't know when I first came across this piece of wisdom — but it fully expresses what I would like to know about anyone before I willingly enter into a partnership with them. And I also think it's what they want to know about me.

The Invitation
Oriah Mountain Dreamer, Indian Elder

It doesn't interest me what you do for a living.
I want to know that you ache for,
and if you dare to dream of meeting your heart's longing.
It doesn't interest me how old you are.
I want to know if you will risk looking like a fool for love,
for your dreams, for the adventure of being alive.
It doesn't interest me what planets are squaring your moon.
I want to know if you have touched the center of your own sorrow,
if you have been opened by life's betrayals or
have become shriveled and closed from fear of further pain.
I want to know if you can sit with pain, mine or your own,
without moving to hide it, fade it, or fix it.
I want to know if you can be with joy, mine or your own,
if you can dance with wildness and let the ecstasy fill you
to the tips of your fingers and toes without cautioning us to be careful,
to be realistic, or to remember the limitations of being human.
It doesn't interest me if the story you are telling me is true.

I want to know if you can disappoint another to be true to yourself,
if you can bear the accusation of betrayal and not betray your own soul.
I want to know if you can be faithful and therefore trustworthy.
I want to know if you can see beauty,
even when it's not pretty everyday,
and if you can source your life from God's presence.
I want to know if you can live with failure, your or mine,
and still stand on the edge of a lake and shout to the silver of a full moon,
"Yes!"
It doesn't interest me where you live or how much money you have.
I want to know if you can get up after a night of grief and despair,
weary and bruised to the bone, and do what needs to be done for the
children
It doesn't interest me who you are, how you came to be here.
I want to know if you will stand in the center of the fire with me and not
shrink back.
It doesn't interest me where or what or with whom you have studied.
I want to know what sustains you from the inside when all else falls away.
I want to know if you can be alone with yourself.
And if you truly like the company you keep in those empty moments.

ABOUT THE AUTHOR

Larry Welke has been selling in the high tech, business-to-business arena all of his adult life, starting with computer sales for IBM and eventually building his own publishing company, International Computer Programs, Inc. (ICP), catering to the computer software and services industry. He has personally taught more than a thousand software sales people over a period of 12 years, principally in the US but also in Europe, South Africa and Japan.

Active in the formation of the first national computer software trade association, he served as President of that group for two years and as Vice Chair and the Chairman of ITAA, the Information Technology Association of America.

He has more than 30 years of experience in writing and public speaking, addressing IT industry audiences throughout the world.

Welke currently lives in Carmel, IN with his wife Janice and serves as President of a closely held information services firm serving both buyers and sellers in the computer software marketplace. He runs the Chicago Marathon each year (but not too fast), plays the occasional game of tennis (but not too well), flies a mean hot-air balloon (but not too high), and is willing to try just about anything — except incest and folk dancing.

Printed in the United States
2652